LET ERIU REMEMBER!

LESSONS AND TEACHINGS
EMBEDDED IN THE MYTHS AND LEGENDS
OF OUR ANCIENT SACRED SITES

EILEEN MCCOURT

Let Eriu Remember!

By Eileen McCourt

This book was first published in Great Britain in paperback during December 2022.

The moral right of Eileen McCourt is to be identified as the author of this work and has been asserted by her in accordance with the Copyright, Designs and Patents Act of 1988.

ISBN: 979-8366362962

CONTENTS

About the Author

Eileen McCourt is a retired school teacher of English and History with a Master's degree in History from University College Dublin.

She is also a Reiki Grand Master teacher and practitioner, having qualified in Ireland, England and Spain, and has introduced many of the newer modalities of Reiki healing energy into Ireland for the first time, from Spain and England. Eileen has qualified in England through the Lynda Bourne School of Enlightenment, and in Spain through the Spanish Federation of Reiki with Alessandra Rossin, Bienstar, Santa Eulalia, Ibiza.

Regular workshops and healing sessions are held in Elysium Wellness, Newry, County Down; New Moon Holistics N.I. Carrickfergus, County Antrim; Angel Times Limerick; Holistic Harmony Omagh, County Tyrone; Celtic School of Sound Healing, Swords, County Dublin; Kingdom Holistic Hub, Mill Road, Killorglin, County Kerry; Reiki Healing Bettystown, County Meath and Moonbeams, Carrigaline County Cork, where Eileen has been teaching the following to both practitioner and teacher levels:

- **Tibetan Usui Reiki levels 1, 2, 3 (Inner Master) 4 (teacher) and Grand Master**

- **Okuna Reiki (Atlantean and Lemurian)**

- **Karuna- Prakriti (Tibetan Usui and Hindu)**

- **Rahanni Celestial Healing**

- **Fire Spirit Reiki (Christ Consciousness and Holy Spirit)**

- Mother Mary Reiki

- Mary Magdalene Reiki

- Archangels Reiki

- Archangels Ascended Masters Reiki

- Reiki Seraphim

- Violet Flame Reiki

- Lemurian Crystal Reiki

- Golden Eagle Reiki (Native North American Indian)

- Golden Chalice Reiki

- Golden Rainbow Ray Reiki

- Goddesses of Light Reiki

- Unicorn Reiki

- Pegasus Reiki

- Elementals Reiki

- Dragon Reiki

- Dolphin Reiki

- Pyramid of Goddess Isis Reiki

- Kundalini Reiki

- Psychic Surgery

Details of all of these modalities can be found on Eileen's website, together with dates and venues of courses and workshops.

This is Eileen's **42nd** book.

Previous publications include:

- **'Living the Magic',** published in December 2014

- **'This Great Awakening',** September 2015

- **'Spirit Calling! Are You Listening?',** January 2016

- **'Working With Spirit: A World of Healing',** January 2016

- **'Life's But A Game! Go With The Flow!',** March 2016

- **'Rainbows, Angels and Unicorns!',** April 2016

- **'........And That's The Gospel Truth!',** September 2016

- **'The Almost Immaculate Deception! The Greatest Scam in History?',** September 2016

- **'Are Ye Not Gods?' The true inner meanings of Jesus' teachings and messages',** March 2017

- **'Jesus Lost and Found',** July 2017

- **'Behind Every Great Man........ Mary Magdalene Twin Flame of Jesus',** July 2017

- **'Out of the Mind and into the Heart: Our Spiritual Journey with Mary Magdalene',** August 2017

- *'Divinely Designed: The Oneness of the Totality of ALL THAT IS'*, January 2018.   Also in **Audiobook**, May 2019

- *'Resurrection or Resuscitation? What really happened in That Tomb?'*, May 2018

- *'Music of the Spheres: Connecting to the Great Universal Consciousness and to ALL THAT IS through the music of Irish composer /pianist Pat McCourt'*, June 2018

- **'Chakras, Crystals, Colours and Drew the Dragon: A child's second Spiritual book'**, July 2018

- *'The Voice of a Master: It is Jesus Himself Who Speaks: Know Thyself'*, December 2018

- *'Kundalini', January 2019*

- *'Brave Little Star Child Comes To Earth'* - Audiobook- April 2019

- *'The Truth will set you free. - Christianity: Where did it all begin?'* May 2019

- *'Titus Flavius Josephus: Did Josephus write the gospels?'* June 2019

- *'Homo SPACIENS: We Are Not From Planet Earth! Our connection with UFOs, ETs and Ancient Civilisations'* August 2019

- *'Those Strange Looking Men In Their Flying Machines: Visitors From Beyond Time and Space? Or From Planet Earth? ETs, UFOs and Who Knows What'* September 2019

- *'I Want to Break Free: Helping our Planet Earth ascend to a higher vibration of Love, Joy, Peace and Happiness for all. We can do it!'* November 2019

- *'The Universe is Mental! Understanding the 7 Spiritual Laws of the Universe, the Hermetic Principles that govern Creation'* January 2020

- *'To Be Or Not To Be.... The Man of Stratford who was never to be Shakespeare: Exposing the deception that was William Shakespeare'* February 2020

- *'If Not Shakespeare, Then Who? Unmasking the Real Bard of Avon! '* April 2020

- *'What On Earth Is Happening? 2020: Year of Balance: Rise of the Divine Feminine'* April 2020

- *'Creating a New World! - Nature WILL be obeyed! - The greatest lesson never taught, but which we need to learn'* May 2020

- *'Humanity's Greatest Challenge? Breaking out of the vortex of ignorance and superstition'* May 2020

- *'Puppets on a String! But! The Strings have been broken! We are free!'* July 2020

- *'Out of the Darkness of Deception and Despair - into the Light of Truth',* February 2021

- *'Lighting the Way: A Little Magic Book of Spiritual Messages and Meanings',* May 2021

- *'Man in the Mirror: Reality or Illusion?'* July 2021

- *'Living Earth: Our Relationship with Mother Nature',* July 2021

- *'The Singing Soul',* July 2021

- *'Finding Sense in the Non-Sense: Seeing the greater picture',* September 2021

- *'Above Our Heads: Predators or Protectors? Extraterrestrials; - The best-kept secret now exposed?* - January 2022

- *'Changing your life - Living the Reiki Way - In Today's World! Just for Today..... '* - January 2022

- *'Dear God.......Where are you?......A Bewildered Soul Talks With God'* - February 2022

- *'You're just a number....and the Universe has it! '* May 2022

and now, this current publication:

- *'Let Eriu Remember! - Lessons and teachings embedded in myths and legends of our sacred sites'*

Podcasts for each of the 42 books can be viewed on Eileen's website and on her author page.

Eileen has also just recently re-published a series of 5 local history books under the title *'Finding Our Way Back'*. These were first published in the 1980s:

Book One: *'Strange Happenings'* - a 1988 collection of local ghost stories and local cures and charms, collected by the students of Saint Patrick's College Armagh.

Book Two: *'Tell Me More, Grandad!'* - a collection of school day memories collected from grandparents and great-grandparents in 1990.

Book Three: *'Gather In, Gather In',* - a collection of children's games and rhymes, 1942-1943, by the late Mr. Paddy Hamill, collected from the pupils in Lislea No 2 Primary School 1939 to 1947 when Mr. Hamill was Principal

Book Four: *'A Peep Into The Past: Armagh in Great-Granny's day'* - Earlier maps of Armagh, explaining how Armagh got its street names, together with photographs of streets and shop-fronts in the early 20th century. Also included is information on schools and education in Armagh in the 19th Century; newspaper articles of interest from 1848; traders in Armagh in 1863 and markets and fairs in Armagh, - of which there were many!

Book Five: *"The Poor Law And The Workhouse In Armagh 1838-1948'* - prepared when Eileen was on secondment in the Public Record Office of Northern Ireland, 1980-1981, under the scholarship scheme provided for teachers by the Department of Education. The resulting publication was used in local schools for coursework for examination purposes. Primary sources include the Armagh workhouse registers and minute books, which are all held in the Northern Ireland Public Record Office in Belfast; government commissions and reports; annual reports of the Poor Law Commission for Ireland 1847-1921, and photographs of the inside and outside of Armagh workhouse, now part of Tower Hill Hospital, taken in 1989 by the late Mary Donnelly (nee Finn), Saint Patrick's College, Armagh.

The recent series of FB weekly videos, *'Our Great Awakening',* together with the previous series *'The Nature of........'* with Eileen and Declan Quigley, Shamanic practitioner and teacher can also be viewed on Eileen's website and on YouTube, together with a series of healing meditations and Shamanic journeys.

Recent Full Moon Meditations with Declan Quigley, Jennifer Maddy and Brenda Murnaghan can be viewed on Eileen's, YouTube channel, - access through website.

Eileen has also recorded 6 guided meditation CDs with her brother, composer/pianist Pat McCourt:

- *'Celestial Healing'*

- *'Celestial Presence'*

- *'Cleansing, energising and balancing the Chakras'*

- *'Ethereal Spirit' - Meditation on the 'I Am Presence'*

- *'Open the Door to Archangel Michael'*

- *'Healing with Archangel Raphael'*

Eileen's first DVD, *'Living the Magic'* features a live interview in which Eileen talks about matters Spiritual.

All publications are available from Amazon online and all publications and CDs are in Angel and Holistic centres around the country, as specified on website.

Please visit also the BLOG page on Eileen's website.

Website: www.celestialhealing8.co.uk

Author page: www.eileenmccourt.co.uk

YouTube channel:

https://www.youtube.com/channel/UChJPprUDnI9Eeu0IrRjGsqw

ACKNOWLEDGEMENTS

Book number *42!*

Sincere thanks are expressed to Francez and Simon Cody of Uisneach, to Kyrie Murray Bard of Tara, to Lar Dooley of Loughcrew, and to Petra Carroll of Emain Macha, for all the information, and for all the fun and laughter we had as we walked and climbed these sacred sites.

A massive thank you also to my faithful and enthusiastic team who have been out on these sites with me in rain, wind and sun, battling up and down hills, over trenches, through **bushes, brambles and briars,** - Declan Quigley, Jennifer Maddy, Brenda Murnaghan, and our intrepid camera woman Kerry O'Hare who goes more than the full mile every time and beyond her own comfort zone. She has disappeared from sight, gone off the radar, has gone down holes and has been ankle deep in sheep dung, all in pursuit of that amazing shot, that *'asked-for'* footage. Thank you Kerry! And thank you to all my team for those memorable times we have had! I love you all to the moon and back.

Thank you to my publishers Dr. Steve Green (Hawk-Eye, - misses nothing!) and Don Hale OBE yet again, for all their work and support, and without whom none of these books would ever actually materialise!

Thank you to all who took part and helped in any way for our Mary Magdalene special event on the 22nd July 2022. What an amazing day we had on Mound Grainne on the Hill of Tara. Thank you to all the singers, all the dancers, all the musicians and all who joined us and contributed in any way to make this event so memorable!

And of course, not forgetting all of you who are buying my books and CDs wherever in the world you are, and all who have taken the time to give me feed-back, and to write reviews for me, both in my books and on Amazon. You are greatly appreciated!

Thank you to all who attend my courses, workshops and meditation sessions, sharing your amazing energies, taking us on such wonderful journeys and through such amazing experiences! We are all so blessed!

And thank you to all of you who have been following me on Facebook. I sincerely hope the posts are bringing some comfort and help to you in these present rapidly changing times when so many people are paralysed with fear and uncertainty.

All is well! All is as it should be!

And as always, I give thanks for all the great blessings that are constantly being sent our way in this wonderful, loving, abundant universe.

Namaste!

8th December 2022 (Full Moon)

FOREWORD

For ancient peoples, stories, myths, legends, parables, fairytales, - all were the normal methods of passing on teachings and lessons. And all passed on through the oral tradition, not the written word. Lessons and teachings passed down to us, all permeated with wisdom and messages to help us along in our daily lives on our spiritual path, and all just waiting to be decoded by us.

Our sacred ancient ceremonial sites, scattered abundantly as they are across our land, - our land of Eriu, - hold the ancient wisdom and knowledge of our ancient ancestors. Our ancient ancestors who were so deeply rooted in the consciousness of Mother Earth, so deeply rooted in the consciousness of cosmology, so strongly inter-connected and balanced within the other diverse realms of existence.

'*And as the story goes.*' - A phrase often repeated throughout this book. Myths and legends abound, passed down orally for generations, and all imbued with truths and teachings that we are meant to find.

A great awakening is underway! Many are yearning for a return to earlier values as they realise the artificial and unsustainable nature of their present lives. As we realise that our ancient ancestors held the wisdom and knowledge that we so desperately need now, and which they passed down to us, in the oral tradition, through the great myths and legends that make up our history.

We are re-engaging with the legacy left to us by our ancient ancestors, through their myths and legends, their megalithic art, - all guiding us back to our very roots, to the wisdom and knowledge that we have forgotten down through the ages, but which we are now re-remembering. We are awakening to the natural energies of our land, the natural energies beneath our feet, embedded in our sacred land, in our sacred sites.

And for the purpose of this book, I have chosen the five sacred sites of Uisneach, Tara, Emain Macha, Loughcrew and Newgrange, simply because they are the ancient sites nearest to me and the most easily accessible from where I live, but there are numerous others, and wherever you happen to live, there are some within easy distance of you. And they all have their myths and legends! Lessons passed down to us from our ancient ancestors - lessons to help us through our daily lives and on our spiritual path. And when we visit these sacred sites, when we spend time there, when we feel that vibrant sacred energy, when we hear those mythical tales, when we see for ourselves that astonishing megalithic artwork on those ancient stones, where each stone has a story to tell, when we see for ourselves those astonishing alignments with the rising and setting sun and with other planets and other star constellations, - all the earth stuff, all the sky stuff, - then we are linking into something wonderful and mind-boggling! We are linking into the wisdom and knowledge of our ancient ancestors, - sophisticated and technologically advanced as they obviously were, with their complex series of solar calendars, defining their year and possibly celestial events. Long-lasting structures, - some over 7,000 years old!

And this is the very reason why these sacred sites must be preserved! Because it is these very same sites, and not our history books that tell us who we really are!

So come with me now through the pages of this book, on a voyage of re-discovery back in time to find the lessons and teachings embedded in the myths and legends of our sacred sites.

Let Eriu remember!

Chapter 1:

Eriu - The naming of our country

Let us start with *remembering* from where we got the name Ireland. Eriu, - Erin, - Eire, - Ireland!

It comes from the name Eriu, - the ancient Earth Goddess of the mythical, mystical Tuatha Dé Danann, - and the name itself means abundant or plentiful. In modern times, Ireland is also known by another version of this same Goddess Eriu's name, - Eire or the poetic name Erin.

Eriu was a daughter of Delbaeth and Ernmas, father and mother respectively, both of the tribe of the Tuatha Dé Danann. The name Tuatha Dé Danann means *'Tribe of the Goddess Danu'* - Danu being the Mother Earth Goddess worshipped from antiquity, - or in its shortened version, Tuatha De, which means *'Tribe of Gods'*.

The Tuatha Dé Danann were a legendary race who held dominion over Ireland in ancient times, and to whom the great passage graves and other monuments are attributed. Through myths and legends they have come to be seen as a supernatural race in their technological prowess, skill in the arts and sciences, and of course in their ability to heal and to perform magic. They have become known as the Shining Ones, the People of Light, the Good People or Na Daoine Maithe, and the People of Peace.

The Tuatha Dé Danann! Mystical, mythical, and permeating Irish stories, myths and legends! And like all myths and legends, there are variations.

We first hear mention of the Tuatha Dé Danann in the *'Lebor Gabala Erenn',* known as the *'Book of Invasions of Ireland',* - an ancient document that tells of successive incursions of peoples into Ireland from the time of the flood down to the millennium before Christianity.

Tom Cowan, in *'Fire in the Head: Shamanism and the Celtic Spirit'*, tells us:

'An atmosphere of magic and mystery surrounds the Tuatha De in the Lebor Gabala (Book of Invasions). We read that they first came to Ireland in obscure clouds, landing on a mountain in the west of the country, and that they caused an eclipse of the sun that lasted for three days. Tradition has it that they were beautiful, handsome beings who arrived in Ireland from the sky on magical sailing ships on the first of May.' (Tom Cowan, *'Fire in the Head'* page 53)

And Judith Nilan in her book *'A Legacy of Wisdom'* writes:

'The Tuatha De were in fact not originally from Ireland, although the primordial nature of their presence renders them indigenous. Their celestial origins remain a matter of much speculation, but there is no dispute their arrival in Ireland was spectacular.' (Judith Nilan *'A Legacy of Wisdom'* page 6)

Anthony Murphy is a journalist, author and photographer from Drogheda, County Louth, near Newgrange, and has studied the astronomy, archaeology and mythology of the Boyne Valley monuments for over 25 years. He has appeared in countless television and radio programmes and has been featured in numerous films and documentaries on the History Channel as a Newgrange expert. In his book '*Newgrange - A Monument to Immortality*' he writes:

'They never really left us, nor were they ever supposed to. The Tuatha Dé Danann are considered by many to be the original gods of Ireland, the earliest divinities who watched over human affairs since the days when we used stones as tools. No invasion, - whether it be a purely mythical one, a religious incursion or a culture-changing imperial assault - could drive the Tuatha Dé Danann completely from the Irish psyche........

They are very much in the otherworld, and there is a notion, expounded in various Irish literature, that they live on side by side with the human inhabitants of Ireland.......

Further to this, a long-standing prophecy of folklore states that they will come out of the sidhe once more, at some time of great need or calamity at some unspecified point in the future.' (Anthony Murphy, '*Newgrange - A Monument to Immortality*' page 163)

The '*sidhe*', referred to above, and according to tradition, were the sacred retreats underground to which the Tuatha Dé Danann fled after they were defeated by the mortal Milesians.

And certainly their arrival on May 1st, Bealtaine, through mists or clouds in magical airships has been a persistent and consistent belief down through the ages.

'With probable origins in another astral or cosmic dimension, it's likely the Tuatha De arrived in Ireland with a very different vibratory signature. And they would soon demonstrate their proficiency with influencing and even manipulating energy fields. It's easy to imagine their personal and collective auras must have been something to behold. As we see throughout religious art history, those who behold this level of

3

spiritual mastery and fluency with spiritual vibrations are often portrayed within a strong halo or light. It's entirely plausible that the Tuatha De wore the mantle of the Shining Ones because their very being glowed and emanated light.' (Judith Nilan, *'A Legacy of Wisdom'* page 8)

Lady Jane Francesca Agnes Wilde, 1821-1896, is probably best known for being the mother of Oscar Wilde, but in her own right she was an Irish poet writing under the pen name Speranza, and supporter of the nationalist movement. She had a special interest in Irish folktales, which she helped to gather, and in her book *'Ancient Legends, Mystic Charms and Superstitions of Ireland',* published in 1887, she writes:

'It is believed by many people that the cave fairies are the remnant of the ancient Tuatha-de-Dananns who once ruled Ireland, but were conquered by the Milesians.

These Tuatha were great necromancers, skilled in all magic, and excellent in all the arts as builders, poets, and musicians. At first the Milesians were going to destroy them utterly, but gradually were so fascinated and captivated by the gifts and power of the Tuatha that they allowed them to remain and to build forts, where they held high festival with music and singing and the chant of the bards. And the breed of horses they reared could not be surpassed in the world - fleet as the wind, with the arched neck and the broad chest and the quivering nostril, and the large eye that showed they were made of fire and flame, and not of dull, heavy earth. And the Tuatha made stables for them in the great caves of the hills, and they were shod with silver and had golden bridles, and never a slave was allowed to ride them. A splendid sight was the cavalcade of the Tuatha-de-Danann knights. Seven-score steeds, each with a jewel on his forehead like a star, and seven-score horsemen, all the sons of kings, in their green mantles fringed with gold, and golden helmets on their head, and golden greaves on their limbs, and each knight having in his hand a golden spear.

And so they lived for a hundred years and more, for by their enchantments they could resist the power of death.' (Lady Wilde, *'Ancient Legends of Ireland'* page 128)

The stories of the Tuatha Dé Danann are all about the universal conflict between the forces of Light and the darker forces, - the Tuatha De being the forces of Light, in conflict with the dark energy forces of both the Fir Bolg and the Fomorians.

'Many stories of the magical powers of the Tuatha De surround the three epic battles. In one story, the three sorceresses of the Tuatha De sent magical showers of fiery rain against the Fir Bolg, causing much damage. In another account of the mythical battle between the divine race of Ireland and the indigenous group of demons, the Formorians, we see magic on a celestial level as Formorian King Bres looks to the west one morning and observes a rising sun.' (Miranda Aldhouse-Green, *'The World of the Druids'* page 126 and quoted in Judith Nilan *'A Legacy of Wisdom'* page 9)

But more about all of this in later chapters! - More about the Fomorians, the Fir Bolgs and the Milesians!

It was to the Tuatha Dé Danann that Eriu, the ancient Earth Goddess belonged - she who gave her name to our country!

Eriu had two sisters, Banba and Fodla. Each of the three sisters married three Kings of Ireland, grandsons of the Dagda: MacGreine, the *'Son of the Sun',* MacCuill, the *'Son of the Hazel',* and MacCecht the *'Son of the*

5

Plough'. Eriu was married to MacGreine.

When the Milesian Celts arrived from Northern Spain, the Tuatha Dé Dannan chose the three sisters, Eriu, Banba and Fodla to negotiate on their behalf, while the Milesians had Amergin, their Bard poet, as their negotiator. As the conflict continued, the three sisters knew that the Milesians were much stronger, and they arranged to meet with them, - and they had only one request, - each asked that when their beloved land would be conquered and taken over, it would be named after her.

And the *'Book of Invasions'*, - 'Lebor Gabala Erenn', - describes how Eriu, Banba and Fodla individually met with Amergin at the top of their own particular sacred mountain. Each of them made the deal with Amergin, but it was Eriu whose request was granted - and so the country would be called after her.

So why Eriu and not Banba or Fodla?

As the story goes, it was Eriu who invited Amergin to the *'sacred marriage'* of a male King to the Goddess of the Land in order to usher in a time of peace and prosperity.

And it was Eriu who had cursed, with powerful words infused with magic, Don Mac Miled, one of the leaders of the Milesian invasion, after he had insulted her, and he drowned shortly afterwards. So Eriu was not to be ignored! After all, she was of the Tuatha Dé Danann!

And it was Eriu whose chosen sacred mound was the Hill of Uisneach, - the mythological and spiritual centre, the *'navel'* of the country.

So it was Eriu who received the privilege of becoming the Goddess of Sovereignty of the Island of Ireland.

However, the names Banba and Fodla are still sometimes used in poetry as names for Ireland. And of course, the name Erin has been used down through history in countless stories and poetry, often in the form of a broken-hearted woman or mother yearning for freedom or lamenting the loss of her children.

So Eriu, a goddess of ancient Ireland, and of the Tuatha Dé Danann, often seen as a personification of the land of Ireland itself, ultimately gave her name to the land of Ireland, the furthest western periphery of Europe.

And from Eriu came the names Eire, Erin, and ultimately Ireland.

Chapter 2:

Mythology and History

And, as we have just seen, the very name of our country comes from mythology! Not from some great historical event or historical person! But from mythology!

It is true, - mythology and history make very uneasy bedfellows. They both pull at us from very different directions.

But where does one end and the other begin? Where does mythology end and history begin? Can we ever tell? Surely they are inextricable?

It was William Butler Yeats who wrote: *'Legend mixes everything together in her cauldron'*. - But could the same not be said about history?

Joseph Campbell wites: *'Myth is much more important and true than history. History is just journalism and you know how reliable that is.'*

And Celtic spiritual teacher Caitlin Matthews explains:

'The mythic present is continually reshaping events, whereas history alone merely chronicles the tides of time. History deprived of its mythic context becomes petrified into sound bites of the timelines; but when myth inspires history, we hear the voices of the past with our own ears, see the images with our own eyes.'

Surely mythology and our legends have made us what we are, as much as what has happened to us down through history? Irish mythology encompasses details of ancient Ireland, with these ancient beliefs passsed down from generation to generation until Medieval times when Christian monks began to write down the narratives and put their own Christian spin on it all and place them into historical records.

History? - All manipulated, all distorted, all fabricated, - depending on which lens you are looking through and from which side of which fence.

History? As James Joyce wrote:

'History is a nightmare from which I am trying to awaken.'

History? - All censored, all written by the winners, by the victors. As Winston Churchill himself said:

'History will be kind to me, for I intend to write it!'

AND HE DID! Yes! - His own version! His own version that found its way into the history books, into the school curriculum, and into world politics! Winston Churchill acknowledging that it is always the victors and never the vanquished who get to write what happened! Put in another way, - as George Orwell said:

'He who controls the past, controls the future, he who controls the present, controls the past.'

This is the blue print for every dictatorship that has ever come to power, and it works simply because any evidence of wrongdoing by the dictator is destroyed.

So history is forever changing! Simply because with the passing of time, the social, political and psychological climate changes, sweeping new ideas are introduced and certain parts of history can be neglected or even rewritten to conform more closely with the new ideals and to support the agendas of those in power.

And myths, legends, fairytales, stories and parables? - They are all simply a means by which ancient peoples passed on oral traditions and taught and gave us lessons, and even though as time goes on, even though the messages and the lessons may be forgotten, the story is still remembered, - until someone further down the line picks up that message again and carries it forward once more.

Myths and legends all come to us multi layered, - just like life itself! First there is the very basic level, the surface level, the ordinary story. Then there are the deeper meanings behind the story, - the lessons, the teachings, the messages being delivered through the oral tradition. Fathomless, again like life itself! Myths and stories told by the ancients to encode a deeper level of knowledge. We just have to look for it! And to understand any of the ancient gods and goddesses, we first need to know the story!

And, just like life too, myths and legends are exciting and mysterious, - not to mention elusive! The mystery of being! The mystery of life!

And all of those stories are about the interplay of the forces of Light and the darker forces, - the continuous battle between what we call good and what we call evil. Right down through the ages, this conflict has featured in all of literature.

Medieval peoples believed that life was an ongoing struggle between good and evil. They strongly believed that good would never defeat evil, as it is not good's way to fight back. Evil was like a whirlwind or a tornado which would spin itself out of energy over time and then good would re-emerge, appearing to be victorious.

And certainly history has proven this! Despite what the history books say, - because remember! - it is always the victors who write the books! - America and Capitalism did not defeat Communism. Communism fell from within! - Just one example of where darkness and negative energy turns in on itself and destroys itself.

And Shakespeare in all of his works reflected this! In all of his plays, there are no evil characters left standing at the end. All are gone, having destroyed each other. All of the characters left at the end are good, with no exception whatsoever - though not all of the good characters are left, - see the big difference here?

It's all about energy again! All energy attracts the same back to itself, like a magnet. Negative energy feeds off more negative energy, positive energy attracts more positive energy. Like to like! But there is an anomaly here! Whilst negative energy attracts more negative energy, it also feeds off good or high energy. Hence we have many good characters in Shakespeare's plays being engulfed and gobbled up by the negative ones, - but not all of them! Yes, negative energy destroys, but it does not destroy all the good. It can destroy some, but not all. The Light will always succeed over the darkness in the end. That's the message coming from the plays of Shakespeare, his plays simply being a means of getting that message across through story telling!

And that is the same message coming from the myths, legends, stories and fairytales. They are not just stories! They are encoded with deeper meanings and embedded with much deeper messages than appears on the surface.

Lady Jane Francesca Agnes Wilde, already referred to in the previous chapter, writes:

'The three great sources of knowledge respecting the shrouded part of humanity are the language, the mythology, and the ancient monuments of a country.

From the language one learns the mental and social height to which a nation had reached at any given period in arts, habits, and civilization, with the relation of man to man, and to the material and visible world.

The mythology of a people reveals their relation to a spiritual and invisible world: while the early monuments are solemn and eternal symbols of religious faith - rituals of stone in cromlech, pillar, shrine and tower, temples and tombs.

The written word, or literature, comes last, the fullest and highest expression of the intellect and culture, and scientific progress of a nation.

The Irish race were never much indebted to the written word. The learned class, the ollamha, dwelt apart and kept their knowledge sacred. The people therefore lived entirely upon the traditions of their forefathers, blended with the new doctrines taught by Christianity; so that the popular belief became, in time, an amalgam of the pagan myths and the Christian legend, and these two elements remain indissolubly united to this day.' (Lady Wilde, *'Ancient Legends Of Ireland'*, page 13)

So surely, the best we can say is that mythology and history blend! There is no demarcating line!

Patrick Weston Joyce, 1827-1914, an Irish historian and writer, known particularly for his research in Irish etymology and local place names in Ireland, wrote:

'Some of the Irish tales are historical, i.e., founded on historical events - history embellished with some fiction; while others are altogether fictitious - creations of the imagination, but always woven round historical personages........

The tales of those times correspond with the novels and historical romances of our own day, and served a purpose somewhat similar. Indeed they served a much higher purpose than the generality of our novels; for in conjunction with poetry they were the chief agency in education - education in the best sense of the word - a real healthful informing exercise for the intellect. They conveyed a knowledge of history and geography, and they inculcated truthfulness, manliness, help for the weak, and all that was noble and dignified in thought, word and action.' (P. W. Joyce, *'The Story of Ancient Irish Civilization',* page 37)

Miranda Aldhouse-Green is Professor Emeritus at Cardiff University. She specialises in the study of shamanism and archaeology of the Iron Age. She has published widely on the Celts and their world, and in her book *'The Celtic Myths'* she writes:

'Myths, like fables, are elusive things. Modern horror films, whether about vampires, ghosts or revived Egyptian mummies, are arguably acceptable because they allow people to explore the darkest aspects of human nature within a safe environment. In a sense, the same is true of myth, but myths are much more complicated. This is in part because they are almost always associated with religious belief - and often magic - and also because contained in mythic tales are answers to some of the most fundamental human concerns: Who are we? Why are we here? Why is our world like this? How was the world created? What happens to us when we die? Myths also explore issues related to human initiation rites: Birth, puberty, marriage and death. Some, particularly those from

the Celtic world, are highly concerned with morality - good and evil, chastity, violence, rape and treachery, war and ethics - with gender-roles, maidenhood, motherhood and virility; and with the ideals of female and male behaviour.

Myths flourish in societies where such issues are not answerable by means of rational explanation. They are symbolic stories, designed to explore these issues in a comprehensible manner. Myths can serve to explain creation, natural phenomena and natural disasters (such as floods, drought and disease), the mysterious transitions of day and night, the celestial bodies and visions of so-called 'holy men', persons (of either gender) with the ability to see into the future and into the world of the supernatural. Myths are inhabited by gods and heroes, and tell of the relationship between the supernatural and material worlds. They can provide divine explanations for the departures of past peoples, their abandoned monuments and burial sites, their houses and places of communal assembly. Myths can explain the origin pf enmities between communities and disputes over territory. Finally, myths are often highly entertaining tales that can while away a dark winter's evening by the fire.' (Miranda Aldhouse-Green, *'The Celtic Myths'* pages 15-16)

And yes, there are indeed such things as mythological truths! Let us now look at some!

Chapter 3:

Mythological truths

Mythological truths? Can there be any such thing? Surely a paradox, an oxymoron, a contradiction?

But not when we consider the previous chapter! Myths and legends were multi layered, and all encoded with knowledge, lessons and teachings passed on in the oral tradition. Encrypted messages left for us within mythological tales, legends, fairytales, ancient sacred sites, poetry, art, numbers and geometry. Messages for us to find and decipher!

Love, compassion, caring, kindness, tolerance, - and at the other extreme, - hatred, fear, anxiety, greed, revenge, jealousy, anger, rage, - all are vibrations of energy, all vibrating on different energy vibration frequency levels! And all the mythological tales, the legends, the fairytales, - all are portals, doors for us into different energy dimensions! They all expose us to these different energy frequencies!

Frank MacEowen has been a lifetime student of indigenous wisdom, dreamwork, and the transformative power of the natural world, - including the seasons and the four directions. In his book *The Celtic Way of Seeing - Meditations on the Irish Spirit Wheel'*, he writes:

'Mythic memory is like a muscle. Exercised, it can become a vital gateway of perception, inspiration, healing, and spiritual connection..........

A myth, or a mythic story, is not just a quaint tale or a form of entertainment (though many Celtic stories can be quite entertaining!) A myth as sacred story is a gift from the past providing an empowered path into the future for us to journey along. Exercising mythic memory stokes a very ancient and intuitive way of knowing - a potent, symbolic, and integrative way of seeing that was known to all our ancestors.

Sacred story can speak to us of timeless lessons (many of them painfully relevant to us in our present age) and offer us different ways of looking at our innermost being.' (Frank MacEowan, *'The Celtic Way of Seeing'* pages 16-17)

Today we are seeing a revival of interest in all things sacred and mysterious, with even the scientific world dedicating serious research time and money to the study.

To the uninitiated, these cultural tales are merely stories, told to children and yet they were designed to be more than this, - much more! We are reminded of truths and levels of consciousness that are beyond the understanding of the logical mind. But when the time is right, for each one of us individually, the soul will stir and then our dormant memory will reawaken!

There is only the one story, the one great universal story! And there has only ever been the one great universal story since the dawn of humanity! The story of the hero! The fascinating story of internal transformation! The painful learning of the lessons we need to learn as we journey towards enlightenment! Heroes are not born. Neither are they bred. They are self-made! They come to self-knowledge, self-realisation through the challenges they face and the way in which they surmount those challenges. The script may change, but the plot remains constant. The self-redeeming hero coming to self-awareness, gaining self-knowledge through overcoming difficulties! The self-redeeming hero facing his darker, lower nature, dying to that nature and being re-born into his higher nature.

As Joseph Campbell explains:

'The images of myth are reflections of the spiritual potentialities of every one of us. Through contemplating these, we evoke their powers in our own lives.' (Joseph Campbell, *'The Power of Myth'* page 258)

And

'By overcoming the dark passions, the hero symbolizes our ability to control the irrational savage within us.' (Joseph Campbell, *'The Power of Myth'* page xiii)

And as Tom Cowan in *'Fire in the Head'* points out:

'Strong evidence that the tales were originally about humans, not deities, is the education and training (the fosterage) of the hero. Although the hero in many tales is presented as a god, his birth, upbringing, and initiation into the mysteries of magic indicate that he or she was not born with such knowledge and skill. The hero had to learn it, like a mortal.' (Tom Cowan *'Fire in the Head'* page 26)

And it is the same story regurgitated down through the centuries. The entry into the dark unknown side of ourselves, facing our darker nature, overcoming that darker lower nature and re-emerging into the light. That is the story of the life of each one of us!

And with every hero there comes a heroine! And vice-versa! Antagonist and protagonist. The masculine and the feminine interplaying! The balancing of the masculine and the feminine energies within each of us! Bringing us to completion!

Each of us is the hero of our own story. We write the script. Each of us is the main actor in our own drama. Each of us plays the starring role in the production of our own life. And therein lies the stuff of heroes! Herein lies the framework for all of literature. That one great universal story!

The well-known fairytales! It is the same theme time and time again. Just different characters, different settings. There never was a Cinderella or a Snow-White! There was no Little Red Riding Hood, no Goldilocks, no Thumbelina, no Jack and the Bean Stalk. They are fictitious characters created to get across certain messages to us. They all face the same trials and tribulations, though in different formats, before achieving happiness, and those trials and tribulations have all got to do with facing the darker side of humanity, that darker, lower nature inside each of us, and overcoming that lower nature.

None of these characters ever existed in real life. They all belong in the field of mythology, in the field of mythological literature, not in the field of history. And what are myths? Myths are made-up stories, created in order to get across a particular message or moral. And we have to find that moral! We have to look beneath the surface!

And what happens in the fairytales, myths and legends and has been regurgitated in the great novels of literature is parallel with what happens to us in real life. It's the one story time and time again! The Brothers Grimm fairytales, the stories of Hans Christian Andersen, the Walt Disney characters, the Irish myths and legends, they are all created around the same theme, the theme of the hero, overcoming difficulties, facing challenges, the challenges of life, coming out of the darkness of his lower nature into the light of his higher nature, involved in the battle between the forces of evil and the forces of good, overcoming the darker forces and thereby redeeming himself.

Those classic fairytales, those fascinating myths and legends, master narratives as they are, are definitely not as child-like as we may often presume! Often brutal, they carry messages, powerful messages! While we can take them at face value and enjoy them simply as entertainment, they are, at the same time and on a deeper level, infused with symbolism and meaning.

To quote Joseph Campbell again:

'Heaven and hell are within us, and all the gods are within us.' (Joseph Campbell *'The Power of Myth'* page 46)

Consider Cinderella for example, or Dorothy in the Land of Oz. Cinderella is mistreated by her wicked step-mother and step-sisters, who make her life difficult and keep her from meeting her Prince Charming. Cinderella's story is a story of personal growth and transformation, as she faces the darkness of the evil of her step-family and learns to distinguish between good and evil, symbolised by the beautiful new dress, which mirrors the change within her, her own inner beauty coming to the fore, a change that signifies that she has reached self-realization and is now ready to meet her prince. Dorothy follows the yellow brick road as she journeys to the Land of Oz, encountering difficult challenges along the way, which she has to surmount, eventually realizing that she had always been able to return home whenever she herself wanted, as she had the power within herself to do so all along. Dorothy's journey is symbolic of the universal quest we all make, looking for wisdom, courage, love, and a sense of home, a sense of belonging. So the morals these stories convey are far more important than the events themselves, and it is the morals for which we have to look, as the morals teach us the lessons.

The witches in the fairytales, often replaced by wicked step-mothers, symbolise the evil force that must be faced, challenged and overcome for the hero or heroine to survive and thrive. This is the crafty and cunning ego within each of us, the ego that must be overcome before we can advance on our Spiritual path. The witch in 'Hansel and Gretel' cunningly tricks the children into believing that she is going to help them by giving them food and a cosy warm bed, only to attempt to eat Hansel. So too, the ego likewise attempts to devour our spirit, our higher nature, our higher being. It is our ego that feeds our desire for and attachment to material possessions, and when it gets us under its control, we are trapped, trapped in just the same way as poor Hansel is trapped in a cage by the witch.

And what would a fairytale be without an enchanted forest? Snow White was left alone in a forest by the woodcutter who was ordered by her wicked step-mother to kill her. The enchanted dark forest is symbolic of those times in our lives when we get lost on our path. At times everything appears dark and depressing for us, such as when we experience the 'Dark Night of the Soul' and we cannot see our way out. Yet it is this very same confusion and fear that offers us the opportunity to face our lower nature and turn our lives around to a more meaningful purpose. Dante, in his 'Divine Comedy' found himself in a dark forest after he lost his way and wandered off the straightforward path.

A forest is symbolic of the feminine or subconscious aspect of us, as the light, the male principle, cannot shine through or penetrate its depths. In order to heal we need to deal with what lies in our subconscious, the bad and the ugly, the darker, the shadow sides of ourselves. That is what life is all about. Preparation for soul enlightenment! If we do not fully engage with everything that we are, the bad and the ugly as well as the good, we fail to 'know thyself', and when we fail to 'know thyself', as I explained in a previous book, '**The Voice of a Master: Know Thyself'**, we cannot become whole, we cannot attain enlightenment or achieve soul ascension. No matter how many good deeds we may do!

And we will no doubt discover, just like Shakespeare's King Lear, that the very poorest beggar, the very least amongst all, the very worst of offenders, all lie within each and every one of us, and that we ourselves are our own worst enemy who most needs our own kindness, compassion and love!

And of course, we have the wolf in the fairytales! The big bad wolf! The wolf in sheep's clothing! Little Red Riding Hood is deceived by the wolf, believing that he is the grandmother. But he represents a sexual predator. The wolf is associated with basic desire and one's lower aspect or nature. He wants to devour or rape pure innocent Little Red Riding Hood and end her Spiritual journey. In her pure innocence, she is unable to distinguish between the goodness of grandmother and the evil of the wolf. Another way of looking at the wolf is as the trickster or schemer, similar to the cat or fox in other tales. These tricksters are often demi-gods in disguise, wise fools who use tricks and cunning as a way of teaching us some particular lesson.

Yes, the fairytales are all about teaching! As too are the Greek myths and legends. Remember, there is only the one universal story!

Consider for example the story of Daedalus and Icarus. Daedalus, in exile in Crete, invented a pair of wax wings to help him escape. Icarus, his son, believed he could fly higher than he actually could, and despite several warnings from his father, he continued to fly towards the sun. The heat from the sun melted the wax on his wings and he fell to his death. Wings symbolise freedom, and putting the wings on Icarus and trusting him to adhere to the instructions for his own safety is symbolic of young people being given their first taste of freedom, their first chance to fly, - it is both dangerous and exhilarating. Icarus' boastfulness in the face of danger was what brought about his death.

Shakespeare's tragic heroes! Macbeth and King Lear! Both examples of where some great person who, through some weakness or flaw in his own character, in the darker side of him, and not facing up to that darker nature, but giving into it, brings about his own downfall and the downfall of those people most closely associated with him.

It's always the same story! The story of our lives! The story of overcoming our darker nature and reclaiming our higher nature, and the consequences which inevitably follow if we fail to do just that!

And the same can be seen in the Irish myths and legends! They too are permeated with symbolism. The symbolism of death, rebirth and life run through all of Celtic mythology, with the magic of the ancient world and nature abounding, - testimony to the power of the mythopoetic language, and in particular the metaphor! As Tom Cowan in *'Fire in the Head'* explains:

'Mythopoetic language, specifically metaphor, has the ability to heal mental and emotional pain because the metaphor mediates the contradictions of life, thus providing a solution that appeals to our

deepest hope that it is possible to transcend the human conditions.'
(Tom Cowan, *'Fire in the Head'* page 97)

'The poet or storyteller in pagan societies was respected and revered for the wisdom and truth the people found in the songs or tales. Poets and singers were thought to have acquired their knowledge and wisdom directly from the gods or spirits. Most cultural mythologies contain an account of how poetry was a gift from the gods or sometimes from a single god or goddess of poetry and inspiration........a key concept in Celtic thinking.....the 'fitness of things', can be found in nature, social relationships, art, and one's personal life.......it is the beauty of cosmic order, the pattern of perfection woven into the fabric of the universe at the creation.' (Tom Cowan, *'Fire in the Head'* page 72-73)

And the early Irish myths are a blend of history and mythology. For example in the story of Saint Patrick banishing the snakes from Ireland. Saint Patrich symbolises the coming of Christianity to Ireland, while the snakes represent the Druids, the pagan culture based on the natural cycles and energies of the earth. Christianity castigated the Druids as heathens, savages and undesirables to be done away with, took over their ceremonial sites and proceeded to build their own churches on those same sites. And why? Because those Druidic ceremonial sites were built on the natural energy lines, the ley-lines of the earth, and the Christians knew that! They even took over Brigid the Druidic goddess of fertility and changed her into Saint Brigid, their own Romanised version, thereby bringing her firmly into the Christian fold.

Irish myths and legends are tales of excitement, daring and magic and are accounts of battles between the forces of good and the more negative forces. Most Celtic tales do not have happy endings. They can be described as bittersweet, regarding happiness as a brief experience.

They remind humans that death is inevitable. The legends also depict inspiring human qualities like faithfulness, soul love, and courage. Besides, they are set in a magical world where anything is possible. Most importantly, Celtic mythology is built on faith in eternal life. The heroes and heroines might die physically, but their souls will live forever in the eternal lands, *'Tir na nog'*. Indeed, death is regarded as a transition to the *'rebirth'* state, the doorway through which the person must pass before becoming immortal.

In the Irish legend of Cuchulain, Cuchulain is the central figure of the Ulster Cycle, a series of tales revolving around the heroes of the Kingdom of Ulster in the early first century. One of these sagas, *'Tain Bo Cuailnge'* (The Cattle Raid of Cooley) is the oldest vernacular tale in western Europe. It tells the tale of our hero, Cuchulain, fighting off the armies of Queen Maeve of Connacht, over a prize brown bull.

Cuchulain was an old, Irish version of the modern-day *'Incredible Hulk'*, terrifying, roused to superhuman rage when faced with wrongdoing or injustice, yet who returns, when the need for anger has passed, to a gentle and sensitive mortal.

It's the same story! It's always the same story! The story of the hero within each of us, the hero that emerges as we dig deep into our lower nature, finding what we never knew we were, finding qualities we never knew we had, bringing those qualities to the surface, making us stronger, preparing us for our eventual spiritual enlightenment.

And today, in William Butler Yeats' poem *'Wandering Aengus'*, we have the same story yet again! Yeats got the inspiration for much of his work from the myths and legends with which he was so familiar.

'Wandering Aengus' is inspired by and based on the legend of the Gaelic

love god Aengus. In the legend, Aengus stirs out of his sleep one night due to a vision of an amazingly beautiful woman. He grows obsessed by her beauty and takes off in wandering, hungering for her love. He discovers her at a lake where she has been changed by magic into a swan, but she changes shape again and disappears.

And what is the lesson?

The lesson is that one can spend one's whole life searching for something, only to realise at the very end, that what they were searching for was within themselves all along. The speaker in the poem has a '*fire in his head*', symbolic of that which motivates him to begin his search. Though he spends his life-time looking for the girl, he grows '*old with wandering*' because every time he catches up with her, she vanishes again. And so on he goes, following her, searching for the '*silver apples of the moon, the golden apples of the sun*', symbolic of that which is unattainable.

And maybe, at the end, there is the suggestion that as he nears the end of his physical life, he realises that what he was searching for all along was already always within him! -

'The place to find is within yourself.' (Joseph Campbell, '*The Power of Myth*' page 203)

So the well known fairytales, the great classical literary novels, the Irish myths and legends all share the same traits. None of them is a true life-story of anyone. They are all made up, imaginative creations, all with the purpose of teaching some specific lesson, some specific lesson that we all need to learn as we travel along the road to spiritual enlightenment, all symbolic of the hero inside each one of us, facing our darker lower nature and eventually, after tough challenges and difficulties, reaching our higher nature, redeeming ourselves, reaching self-awareness, gaining self-knowledge, coming to '*know thyself*', and eventually attaining spiritual enlightenment.

The stories of the ancient gods and goddesses, - and the stories in the Christian Bible, - they too all belong in the field of mythology, in the field of mythological literature, and not in the field of history. They all describe events which never happened, people who were never there, events and people created and made up by their authors to get across certain lessons to us, certain lessons that we need to learn on our Spiritual journey towards enlightenment, towards full ascension.

Judith Nilan:

'This is the call of our ancestors....... and if we listen for it, the call of our soul. It is a call to know, honour and celebrate ourselves as part of a mystical and universal cosmology. It is a call to live into our potential as co-creators with the sacred and have the harmony manifest in our lives. There are as many ways to answer the call as there are people who hear it - for while this is perhaps the most important work we will do in life, it is at the same time individually and uniquely ours. The journey of soul is one we walk alone. Yet it is a path that has been walked by countless others through generations of Irish history, leaving behind a legacy of wisdom. As we encounter their stories, their music, poetry and song, we touch the divine harmony that has lived and continues to live in the land and the people of Ireland. Their legacy offers inspiration and insight for our own journey. And in this journey of remembering and re-remembering we come back to the truth and harmony of ourselves.' (Judith Nilan, '*A Legacy of Wisdom*' page 46)

There is no '*Incredible Hulk*', no '*Spider Man*', no '*Popeye and Olive*' in real life! They are made-up characters to get across a message! And the story is built around them!

There is only the one universal story! The story of the rise of the hero within each one of us, as we face our lower nature and surmount the challenges and difficulties that all of this process entails, fighting our way through the darkness, before we can emerge into the light as fully completed beings.

It may be a different age, a different culture, it may be different characters in a different setting, but the symbolism is always the same, and the lessons are always the same. It is always the story of the human struggle that goes on inside each one of us, the struggle to become the hero in the stage production of our own life, the struggle to defeat our lower nature and emerge from the darkness into our higher nature.

And we must all work our way through the darkness to get to the light!

There can be no other way!

Chapter 4:

The sacred marriage of the mortal king and the immortal Land Goddess

Before we consider the lessons and teachings in myths and legends associated with various sacred sites in Ireland, we need to consider the position of a king in society, as these kings permeate all of our myths and legends!

For our ancient ancestors, society was tribal, rural, hierarchal and familiar. The two pivotal institutions were the *'fine'* or *'deirbfhine'* - the family group or social unit, - and the *'tuath',* - the territorial or political unit or petty kingdom. Translating these terms as just family, tribe or clan is very misleading, as society in ancient Eriu was much more complex than this!

Ancient Ireland was not so much one country, but a number of these small, distinct kingdoms or *'tuatha',* each with its own king, - referred to in the ancient annals as a *'Ri tuath',* and there could have been as many as one hundred and fifty separate tuatha, each with up to a few thousand inhabitants. There were also the higher-ranking kings, known as the *'Ri cuaige'* meaning king of one-fifth, as Ireland in ancient times had five provinces, - Ulster, Munster, Leinster, Connaght and Meath or Midhe, the middle province. Much indeed is written in legends and myths of the *'Ard Ri'* or High King in ancient Ireland, but the highest degree of kingship referred to in the early annals is the *'Ri cuaige',* - king of one fifth, king of a province, - and at any one time there were five of these, all trying to be acknowledged as the **'Ard Ri'.**

There was actually no organic connection between these two units - the **fine** and the **tuath.** The fine, - the family group - included all relations in the male line of descent for five generations, corresponding to the Hindu *'joint-family',* and in it was invested the ultimate ownership of family land - **'fintiu'.** This was the normal family group, basically the relationship between a man and his brothers, but it was extended over five generations to include his own children, his father's brothers, his grandfather's brothers, and even his great-grandfather and his brothers.

When someone within the *fine* died without any immediate heirs, his property was distributed evenly among his more distant relatives. The individual as such had few or no legal rights, all being contingent on his membership of the *fine*. There was no system of primogeniture, - land was shared equally between brothers, and the head of the senior line was the **'cenn fine',** who represented the family in all its affairs.

Even in the case of royal families and the kingship, there was no primogeniture. Each member of the king's *'deirbfhine'* was theoretically a **'rigdamnae'** - eligible to be elected king. A **'tanaiste ri'** would be elected during the king's lifetime in order to avoid bloodshed at his death between rival contestants.

And the king himself was expected to be flawless and unblemished:

'No person not of age, stupid, blind, deaf, deformed, or otherwise defective in mind or body, or for any reason whatsoever unfit to discharge the duties of the public position, or unfit worthily to represent the manhood of the community, could be chosen for the king or could hold the kingship; even a blemish on the face was disqualification. Here

were requirements enough, positive and negative, which not every man could satisfy.' (Laurence Ginnell. *'The Brehon Laws'* page 67.

The king was married to the sacred land, the land of Eiru herself, and his position was a sacred gift, - the marriage of the mortal ruler and the immortal Goddess of the land. Failure on his part to live up to expectations of his position would result in disaster for all concerned. The main signs that the king was unfit to rule were seen in defeat in battle, sickness amongst the people, dryness of cows, disease in animals, blight in the crops or scarcity of corn.

To be considered acceptable to the Goddess Eriu, the king had to be not just physically unblemished, but be possessed of the noble qualities of reputation and dignity befitting a goddess, - hospitality, righteousness, warfare, generosity, geniality, justice, courtesy, glory, bravery and discernment.

A big ask and a big demand! But it was as it was!

The late Murt MacGarraidhe, 1960-2006, in his book *'Strangers at Home'* published in 2009 writes:

'The king had no despotic powers and few privileges and he could be deposed by popular will. His responsibilities to the community were onerous, because his office was a sacred one and if he should renege on propriety nothing but disaster would ensue during his reign. The king had to remain acceptable to the Land of Eire herself, or to that personification of her that was present in his tuath. His inauguration as king was seen and understood as a marriage of the king to the lands, the patrimony of his people.

The king's pleasing presence could then intercede with the forces of nature and with the supernatural, over which his people had no control, but on which their prosperity depended.' (Murt MacGarraidhe, *'Strangers at Home'* page 130)

And MacGarraidhe explains how the leadership of the king, the qualities he was expected to have, - known as the *'Justice of a King',* - and the well-being of the sacred Land and the people were inextricably linked, as in the following account he gives of King Conare:

'It is clear to those who consider well, how profitable to the world is the justice of a king, for it is the peace of peoples, the security of country, the safety of the common folk, the defence of the tribe, the cure of illness, the joy of men, the clemency of the weather, the calm of the seas, the fruitfulness of the earth, the consolation of the poor, the inheritance of children, for the king himself, the hope of future bliss.' (Taken from Frances J. Byrne, *'Irish Kings and High Kings,* The Four Courts Press, 1973, 2001, pps. 25-26: citing *De Duodecem Abusivis Saeculi*, a seventh century religious treatise by an anonymous Irish writer which contains a chapter on *Rex Iniquus* (*The Unjust King*) and quoted in MacGarraidhe *'Strangers at Home'* page 131)

'There was great bounty, then, in Conare's reign: seven ships being brought to Inber Colptha in June of every year, acorns up to the knee every autumn, a surfeit (of fish) over the Buas and the Boand (Boyne) each June, and an abundance of peace, so that no one slew his neighbour anywhere in Eriu ......from the middle of spring to the middle of autumn, no gust of wind stirred any cow's tail ; there was no thunder, no stormy weather in Conare's reign.' (Taken from Geoffrey Gantz (Trans), *Early Irish Myths and Sagas; The Destruction of Da Derga's Hostel*; Penguin Classics, London, 1981, p. 67 and quoted in MacGarraidhe *'Strangers at Home'* page 131)

31

'It is through the justice of the ruler that many creatures and many animals from the deep and great seas are cast up on lawful shores.' (Taken from Fergus Kelly, *Early Irish Farming,* School of Celtic Studies, Dublin Institute for Advanced Studies, 2000, p. 284 and quoted in MacGarraidhe *'Strangers at Home'* page 131)

'It is through the justice of the ruler that abundance of fish swim in streams.' (Taken from Fergus Kelly, *Early Irish Farming,* School of Celtic Studies, Dublin Institute for Advanced Studies, 2000, p.286. Citing tenet of *Audacht Morainn*; 600-700 and quoted in MacGarraidhe *'Strangers at Home'* page 131)

'It is through the justice of the ruler that abundance of great tree fruit of the great wood are tasted.' (Taken from Julia H. Smith, *Europe after Rome - A New Cultural History 500-1000:* Oxford University Press, 2005; p. 246. Citing *Audacht Morainn*; 600-700, and quoted in MacGarraidhe *'Strangers at Home'* page 131)

MacGarraidhe also gives an example of the consequences when the standards expected of a king were broken, as in the case of King Conaire Mor of Tara:

'They passed Uisnech Mide, and after that, they saw forays being made from north and east and west, troops and hosts in turn, and naked men, and the land of the Ui Neill was a cloud of fire above them.

'What is this?' asked Conaire.

'Not difficult that', replied his people. 'When the land burns, it is easy to see that the law has been broken.' (Taken from Annette Jocelyn Otway-Ruthven, *A History of Medieval Ireland*; Routledge, 1980, p. 13 and quoted in Murt MacGarraidhe *'Strangers at home'* page 133)

Another scenario in which the Land made known her displeasure with a king is also found in MacGarraidhe. This situation involves King Cormac Mac Airt, when his expedition into the territory of Munster was seen as unjust and the ground itself refused to accept the poles of his tent, and so rejecting his presence and his claim of lordship over the lands and the peoples there. And as the story goes, the Druids and the Tuatha Dé Danann, both so skilled in magic, were powerless in the face of the land of Eriu herself:

'It was there that Cormac said: 'Now Cith Rua, erect my tent as you were wont to erect the tents of my father and my grandfather, for I will not leave here until my taxes are either paid or withheld'. Cith Rua then tried to drive an alder post into the ground for the erection of the tent but neither grass nor earth would receive the tent pole from him. Cith Rua was defeated in his efforts to drive the tent pole into the earth and Cormac exclaimed: 'Woe and misfortune to you, O Cith Rua, what has become of your strength that you cannot insert the pole? For the hill is not allowing the tent pole into it, it is like trying to penetrate a rock.'

'It is not that I haven't the strength to insert it', said Cithn Rua, 'It is because of the attempted injustice that this rejection has occurred.'

'Listen to what the old Druid says, O Colpa', said Cormac. 'He failed to erect the tent, now you erect it yourself.'

Colpa took the tent pole in his hand and he began to censure and revile Cith Rua. He set about the work with enormous energy and his body was so stretched that middle-aged men could pass between every two of his ribs. He drove the stake against the ground but the earth would not accept it. So forceful were his efforts that the stake broke into fragments.' (Taken from Sean O Duinn, Editor and Translator, *Forbhais*

Droma Damhghaire / The Siege of Knocklong, taken from the *Book of Lismore*, Mercier Press, Cork, 1992, p. 41-43 and quoted in Murt MacGarraidhe, *'Strangers at Home'* page 89)

Irish historian Patrick Weston Joyce, 1827-1914, and already referred to in a previous chapter, wrote:

'The highest people in the land, even kings and queens, had to submit to the laws, exactly the same as common subjects; and if a king was wronged, he had to appeal to the laws, like other people. ' (P. W. Joyce, *'The Story of Ancient Irish Civilization'* page 13)

And as an example of this, Joyce relates the story about a case of trespass on a queen's ground, which was tried in court:

'In those days there reigned at Tara a king named MacCon, whose queen had a plot of land, not far from the palace, planted with glasheen, i.e., the wood-plant, for dyeing blue. In the neighbourhood there lived a female brewy, or keeper of a hostel for travellers, who had flocks and herds like all other brewys. One night a flock of sheep belonging to her broke into the queen's grounds and ate up or destroyed the whole crop of glasheen; upon which the queen summoned her for damages.

In due course the case came before the king (for the queen would not appear before an ordinary brehon), and on hearing the evidence he decided that the sheep should be forfeit to the queen to pay for the crop. Now, although the glasheen was an expensive and valuable crop, the sheep were worth a great deal more; and the people were enraged at this unjust sentence; but they dared not speak out, for MacCon was a usurper and tyrant.

Among the people who dwelt in Tara at this time was a boy, a handsome, noble-looking young fellow, whom the people all knew by the name of Cormac. But no one in the least suspected that he was in reality a prince, the son of the last monarch, Art the Solitary, who had been slain in battle by the usurper, MacCon. He was wise and silent, and carefully concealed from all who he was; for he well knew that if he was discovered the king would be sure to kill him.

While the trial was going on he stood behind the crowd listening quietly; and being by nature noble and just-minded, even from his youth up, he could not contain himself when he heard the king's unfair and oppressive sentence; and he cried out amid the dead silence: - 'That is an unjust judgment! Let the fleeces be given up for the glasheen - the sheep-crop for the land-crop - for both will grow again!'

The king was astonished and enraged, and became still more so when the people exclaimed with one voice: 'That is a true judgment, and he who has pronounced it is surely the son of a king!'

In this manner the people, to their great joy, discovered who Cormac was. How he managed to escape the vengeance of the king we are not told; but escape he did; and after a time the usurper was expelled from Tara and Cormac was put in his place. To this day Cormac MacArt is celebrated in Irish records as a skilful lawyer and writer on law, and as the wisest and most illustrious of all the ancient Irish kings.' (P. W. Joyce, *'The Story of Ancient Irish Civilization'* page 13-14)

So the king was not above the law, which he was indeed expected to observe at all times. He was there to make wise decisions, and always to put the good of his people first.

And as the story goes, and as we read in chapter 1, it was Eriu who invited Amergin to the *'sacred marriage'* of a male King to the Goddess of the Land in order to usher in a time of peace and prosperity.

Chapter 5

Mythological and sacred Uisneach

The Hill of Uisneach is considered to be the mythological and spiritual Centre of Ireland, and if you look at it on a map it truly looks to be the centre of the land. In the past it was believed that Uisneach was a gateway to the Otherworld, and that it holds the four provinces of Ireland together. It is a place for druids to meet, and is heavily associated with the festival of Bealtaine.

And again, we have history and mythology intermingling, all interwoven, impossible to separate.

So what are the myths and legends associated with Uisneach? And what are the lessons and teachings embedded within them?

Let us start with the ancient Goddess Eriu and the God Lugh!

Eriu and Lugh

Eriu, the Earth Goddess, who, as we saw in the first chapter, gave her name to our country, was the Triple Goddess - a trinity of three distinct aspects or figures united in one being. The Triple Goddess in mythology is representative of the three stages in the female life cycle, - the Maiden, the Mother and the Crone. Our ancient ancestors saw Ireland and the land as the Mother Spirit, - alive, living, breathing, - and so Eriu, being the Triple Goddess, is Eriu, Banba, the beautiful young maiden, and finally Fodla. Eriu, Banba and Fodla, - three sisters. Eriu awakens and comes alive as Banba at Spring time, when the seeds are sown; then the beautiful young maiden becomes Eriu, the woman with child, and then during the harvest season she becomes Eriu the mother, and so on into the cold winter season, when Eriu becomes Fodla, the Crone, - the old woman of winter where we rest and nurture ourselves. Then into spring and Banba again, - and so the cycle continues.

Tom Cowan in '*Fire in the Head*' writes:

'*The fascination with threes is widespread in Celtic art and literature, both on the continent and in the British Isles. Celtic sculptors often group figures in threes, or sculpt one figure with three heads, or one head with three faces.........*

Celtic deities appear in much the same manner. With a profound and enduring love of threes, the Celts imagined their gods and goddesses in three-somes. The three Brigids, the three Mothers, the three war goddesses - Morrigan, Macha and Bodb (collectively called the Morrigan) - are important Celtic goddesses.' (Tom Cowan. '*Fire in the Head*' page 68)

About the power of three, Miranda Aldhouse-Green writes:

'*Three seems to have been a sacred number in both Irish and Welsh tradition. In Irish mythic legends, the battle-goddesses variously called the Morrigna (singular Morrigan), the Badbh and Macha occur (like the witches in Shakespeare's 'Macbeth' in triple form. In the Irish pantheon, there were three craft-deities: Giobhniu, Luchta and Creidhne. The personification of Ireland itself was also presented as three goddesses: Eriu, Fodla and Banbha. The Ulster hero Cú Chulainn wore his hair in three braids and killed his enemies in threes.*' (Miranda Aldhouse-

Green, '*The Celtic Myths*' page 30)

And Green quotes from the '*Tain Bo Cuailne*' about Cú Chulainn:

'*Cú Chulainn reached Forgall's rampart and gave his salmon-leap across the three enclosures to the middle of the fort. In the inner enclosures he dealt three strokes at three groups of nine men. He killed eight men at each stroke and left one man standing in the middle of each group. They were Emer's three brothers, Scibar and Ibor and Cat.*'

And Eriu, Banba, Fodla, - the Triple Goddess, Mother Earth herself, as our ancient ancestors saw it, rests here at Uisneach.

And what about Lugh? Lugh, the Sun God and King of the legendary Tuatha Dé Danann!

The name Tuatha Dé Danann, as we saw in the first chapter, means the people of the God Dana. Ancient Ireland was divided into areas called *tuatha or* territorial divisions, - equivalent roughly to what we call townlands, - and *fine* or family division, with every person belonging to both a tuath and a fine. And as we saw in chapter 4, the kingship of each tuath was not automatically passed from father to son. Back in those ancient times, the kingship was a bitterly fought contest between all the Ri Domnaigh, - heirs or possible successors - and these included all the males in the Fine. Whoever proved himself the strongest, the bravest and the most worthy, - as in battle, or in cattle raids, especially those carried out in broad daylight, - then he would be the new king.

So where does Lugh come into the story? Who was this Lugh? Lugh, who defeated Balor and the Fomorians at the Battle of Moytura.

And who was Balor? And who were the Fomorians?

In the Irish myths of the battles of Moytura, where the Tuatha Dé Danann fought the Fomorians, we are told that this Lugh, who appeared so mysteriously at the battle, impressed the King of the Tuatha Dé Danann so much with his fighting skills that the king handed over the kingship to Lugh, believing this young stranger to be a better warrior, and therefore more qualified to be king of the Tuatha De Danaan. Hence Lugh became king of the Tuatha Dé Danann.

And Balor?

Balor was Lugh's grandfather. Known as Balor of the Evil Eye, - he led the Formorians, a group of malevolent supernatural beings, demonic creatures, and the enemies of the Tuatha Dé Danann. Tom Cowan in *'Fire in the Head'* writes about the Fomorians:

'The Fomorians dwelt in Ireland before the arrival of the Dananns. They seem to have been present always, if not on the land itself, then lurking in their strongholds offshore in the northern seas. They were thought to be more ancient than the gods. Huge, hideous, misshapen beings, they were the powers of darkness, night, chaos, monstrous births, the antithesis of day, light, order, and human beauty. Deformed creatures, they appeared to have only one leg and one arm. Their chieftain, Balor of the Evil Eye, had a gigantic eye that burned to ashes whatever it gazed upon. Usually he kept it closed beneath a mercifully heavy lid that required several men to lift open. Balor's Eye was a powerful weapon against their adversaries.

Although the Fomorians are often portrayed as cosmic evil, a more sympathetic interpretation depicts them as the nonhuman deities who control fertility, the untamed spirits of the land, and the destructive forces of nature, such as storms, quakes, blight, and drought. As such,

*they cannot be totally destroyed nor viewed as totally evil, since even
the natural forces that harm human society play a vital role in the
grander scheme of things.'* (Tom Cowan, *'Fire in the Head'* pages 52-53)

As a leader of the Fomorians, Balor ruled in Ireland before the arrival of
settlers. He was a very powerful but also tyrannical ruler, commonly
associated with terror and fear, which paralysed the Irish people. Balor
had his own weapon of mass destruction, - a huge eye, which when
opened, wreaked destruction and death with a poisonous gaze, capable
of slaying an entire army when that eye was turned on them. A bit like
the Greek Medusa who also had the ability to deal the death card in
similar manner.

The eye was always covered with seven very heavy eyelids or cloaks,
keeping it cool and safe and four strong men were needed to lift them
up. When the eyelids were taken off one by one, the eye could strike
down all it looked upon and the whole land caught fire. The eye was
constantly closed and used only against enemies on the battlefield.

And how had Balor's eye come to be so powerful?

According to a legend, one day, Balor had spied on some Druids who
were preparing a potion of knowledge and wisdom. Some of the
magical potion splashed out and hit him in the eye. The substance
penetrated Balor's eye and gave it magical power. Tradition also has it
that in older age, Balor's eye became exhausted and its eyelid had to be
hoisted up by his servants with ropes and lifters.

Balor himself feared no man or no enemy, But one thing terrified him
and was his only weakness, - the ancient prophecy and fate one cannot
escape! According to the prophecy, and the story, Balor himself would
eventually be slain by his own grandson, - so in an attempt to trick fate,

Balor decided to imprison his own daughter, Ethniu, in a tower on Tory Island away from all contact with men. Thus, she could never become pregnant and Balor's life would be safe.

But once again fate proves impossible to escape. And here we have another of those metaphorical messages embedded in the myths! - *FATE!*

Balor's own greed contributed also to his downfall, for he stole a magical cow of fertility, the Glas Ghaibhleann, which had the ability to produce never-ending and copious amounts of milk. According to one version of the story, the magical cow belonged to Cian the Mighty, a member of the Tuatha Dé Danann. To retrieve the prized animal, Cian had to come up with a plot of revenge. And look at the interplay of greed and revenge here! - Embedded in all the metaphors!

Cian knew the Druids' prophecy about Balor's death from the hands of his own grandson and he also knew why Balor had locked his daughter, Eithne, in a tower, where she was strictly guarded by twelve matrons, preventing her from ever seeing a man. Disguised as a Druidess, Cian entered the stronghold where Eithne lived and seduced her. The fruitful relationship resulted in three children but when Balor discovered the trick, he ordered the three children to be drowned in the sea. Only one child, Lugh, survived and was secretly raised in difficult times of continuous conflict between the Danaans and the Fomorians, - those demonic creatures ruled by the tyrannical King Balor.

And this was the same Lugh who appeared so mysteriously at the Battle of Moytura (Magh Tuiredh).

Despite being half-Fomorian, Lugh fought on the side of the Tuatha de Danann and he played an important role in the Fomorians' downfall.

Balor struck down many Tuatha de Danann and he could conquer them all, but first, he had to meet his grandson, Lugh, and confront his skills with his deadly eye. He ordered his servants to pull up the eyelids and while his deadly eye was partially open, and as Lugh saw it opening, he chose his perfect moment to attack it. He shot a sling-stone that drove the eye out the back of Balor's head, slaying Balar and casting the poisonous glare onto the Fomorians themselves. So Lugh won the battle.

Or so the story goes!!

The incident wreaked chaos among the Fomorian soldiers and fulfilled the prophecy saying that Balor would die one day, at his grandson's hand. It is said that even as Balor lay on the ground, his evil eye was so strong that it killed twenty-seven of his own Fomorian warriors who looked at it.

Remember how I explained earlier about how myths and legends are all about passing on through stories some particular lesson or deeper meaning? So what is the deeper meaning encoded in the legend of Lugh and Balor?

And here is where those of us who love metaphors and symbolism have a field day!

It's all about the interplay of greed and desire for revenge with Balor and the Fomorians representing the power of darkness, evil and death. Balor's evil eye is metaphorical for the wave of negativity, darkness and fear that can sweep over us at any time in our lives, threatening to engulf and destroy us. But when we find ourselves in this situation, we must gather all our strength to try and withstand it and find a way to turn that evil and darkness back in on itself again, - destroying it.

And all of Shakespeare's evil characters destroy themselves! Lear, Macbeth, etc - the message being that evil feeds off evil and eventually spins itself out of energy and destroys itself. Evil turns upon itself! Don't get caught up in it! But it is exactly that shadow that provokes us into action! The darkness before the light! All metaphorical!

But to continue the story of Lugh! - It was at Lough Lugh here at Uisneach, 600 feet above sea level, and 10,000 years old, that legend tells us Lugh met his mortal end.

And how did that happen?

As the story goes, - Lugh, the Sun God of the Tuatha Dé Danann, the King of Ireland, was slain by the three sons of Ciarmuid, King of Leinster - McKill, McCairt, and MacGreinne, and as the story further goes, it was because Lugh's wife was involved in an affair or a dalliance, with Ciarmuid, King of Leinster. Lugh, in a fit of anger and jealousy, went to Ciarmuid, challenged him and killed him.

And the message embedded here in the extended metaphor?

By killing Ciarmuid, Lugh showed his failings and his flaws, - the King was supposed to be flawless, as we saw in chapter 4, - he was married to the Goddess of the Earth and therefore supposed to be beyond blemish. Lugh should not have given into his jealousy and anger. It only led to his demise!!

And how did his demise come about?

Back to the story again! - Lugh came back to Uisneach and at the feast of Bealtaine as he stood by Lake Lugh, the three sons of Ciarmuid approached from the East, from Leinster, coming to find Lugh and to seek revenge for the death of their father. McGreinne was the greatest spear-thrower in Ireland, and he flung his spear at Lugh, which stuck into Lugh's left foot, pinning him to the ground. The three ran at Lugh, picked him up and flung him into the lake, where he drowned in front of all the people. The people were devastated, not just because Lugh, their king, was dead, but also because he had been taken from them by three of their own, - and all because of jealousy and desire for revenge. And here is the lesson in this mythological tale!

Lugh's body was taken from the lake and it is said that he was laid to rest in the early bronze age cairn behind the lake, Cairn Lugdach.

So Uisneach, it is said, is the resting place of Kings, Gods and Goddesses.

The King's Palace

The area known as the King's Palace lies on the mound just outside of the main Uisneach hill area. It was called the King's Palace because in ancient times, this was where the king stayed during the great festivities when tens of thousands of people would have made their way to the sacred sites, for the four main festivals of Samhain, Imbolg, Bealtaine and Lughnasa, and also the four festivals of the equinoxes and solstices.

The King's Palace is composed of two concentric circles, clearly visible from the air, - the lemniscate, the Infinity Sign, the figure 8, - just as we find on Tara and on Emain Macha, and which I will deal with in greater detail in chapter 10.

The ancient path travelled by those coming from the south to Uisneach is clearly visible, and leads directy to the larger of the two concentric circles. Just beyond the node, - the joining point, - we have the smaller circle, and it is here where the king and his immediate family would have stayed. Temporary dwellings would have been erected, made of nearby rushes or whatever materials would have been available, and these would either have been dismantled again at the end of the festivities or left standing and built upon again on the next festive occasion.

The larger circle was where the king's extended family would have stayed, along with the bards, poets, musicians and other entertainers. And then down around the bottom of the mound and stretching out into the distance, the ordinary people would have erected their shabby tents or whatever they had, and positioned themselves for the several days that the festivities ensued.

And why were the nobles, bards and musicians up at the top of the mound, alongside the king?

Ancient Ireland was structured hierarchically, from the king downwards clearly divided into different levels. The ancient manuscript the **'Senchus Mor',** meaning the *'Great Ancient Tradition',* is a collection of ancient Irish laws. Compiled in the fifth century, it is a record of the customary law of the ancient Irish, and is one of the most important legal texts from early Ireland. The Senchus Mor tells us the noble class were next to the king in priority, - possessing considerable land, livestock and other property, - and distinguished from each other by the number of clients each had, - clients being those people to whom the nobles granted land and cattle in return for services. This noble class also included the poets, bards, brehons, and musicians, as great gifts and knowledge were highly prized. As was craftmanship, such as that of blacksmiths and goldsmiths. And we see this in the tale of Cuchulainn where the blacksmith Culain invited King Conor to a feast at his house near Emain Macha.

Lady Wilde writes:,

'The Irish kings in ancient times kept up splendid hospitality at their respective courts, and never sat down to an entertainment, it was said, without a hundred nobles at least being present. Next in rank and superb living to the royal race came the learned men, the poets: they were placed next the king, and above the nobles at the festivals, and very gorgeous was the appearance of the Ard-File on these occasions, in his white robes clasped with golden brooches, and a circlet of gold upon his head...........

A train of fifty minor bards always attended the chief poet, and they were all entertained free of cost, wherever they visited, throughout Ireland, while the Ard-File was borne on men's shoulders to the palace of the king, and there presented with a rich robe, a chain, and a girdle of gold. ....

..........The poets, above all men, were required to be pure and free from all sin that could be a reproach to learning. From them was demanded: Purity of hand; Purity of mouth; Purity of learning; Purity of marriage; and any poet who did not preserve these four purities lost half his income and his dignity, the poet being esteemed not only the highest of all men for his learning and intellect, but also as being the true revealer of the supreme wisdom.' (Lady Wilde, *'Ancient Legends, Mystic Charms and Superstitions of Ireland'*, page 213)

Satire was the favoured technique of the poet, - the **'Ollamh'**, - as Tom Cowan in *'Fire in the Head: Shamanism and the Celtic Spirit'* points out:

'The malicious insult enjoys a distinguished history in Celtic society. Among the poet's magical powers was the ability to compose a satire that would bring ruin upon the subject, reshape the landscape, control the elements, and influence animals. Kings especially feared the poet's satire for it could cause them to lose their right to rule. An early Irish tradition claims that highly trained poets had once been judges, and were therefore experts on the rights and duties of kings.' (Tom Cowan, *'Fire in the Head: Shamanism and the Celtic Spirit'* pages 88-89)

There were in fact seven grades of poet recognised, as we learn from the ancient manuscript *'Senchus Mor'*:

'The Ollamh with his seven times fifty stories, the Anruth with his thrice fifty and half fifty, the Cli with his eighty, the Cana with his sixty, the Dos with his fifty, the Mac-fuirmidh with his forty, the Fochluc with his thirty, the Drisac with his twenty, the Taman with his ten stories, and the Ollaire, with his seven stories. These were the chief stories and the minor stories. The chief stories which they repeated, treated of demolition, cattle-spoils, courtships, battles, killings, combats, elopements, feasts, encampments, adventures, tragedies, and plunderings.' (*'Senchus Mor'* and quoted in Jo Kerrigan *'Brehon Laws: The Ancient Wisdom of Ireland'* page 50-51)

So the bards were held in high esteem! And placed next to the king! As we see at Uisneach!

Also on the King's Palace mound, next to the larger circle where the nobles, bards and the king's extended family would have stayed, there is a site on which there appears to have been a dwelling, which would have had timber uprights, creating a surrounding wall, and a roof, and the entire space would have been shared with the family and the animals, - animals being the main form of wealth! There is a gap clearly visible between two trees, and this obviously would have been an entrance to this part of the mound, and beyond that, another ancient roadway, - and this roadway leads straight to the Hill of Tara.

Lady Wilde in *'Ancient Legends of Ireland'* writes:

'.....our wealth was our cattle; our wars were for our cattle; the ransom of our chieftains was in cattle; our taxes were paid in cattle; the price paid for our most valuable manuscripts was so many cows. Even in comparatively modern times, our battle cloaks were made of leather; our traffic and barter were the Pecuaniae of our country; and the 'Tain-bo-Cuailne', the most famous metrical romance of Europe, after the 'Niebelungenlied', is but the recital of a cattle raid from Connaught into Louth during the raeign of Maeve, Queen of Connaught - a personage transmitted to us by Shakespeare, as Queen Mab of the 'Midsummer Night's Dream'..........

The Boromean, or cattle tribute, which the King of Tara demanded from the Leinstermen, was perhaps the cause of the greatest intestinal feud which ever convulsed so small a space of European ground for so great a length of time. This triennial cattle tax, besides 5,000 ounces of silver, 5,000 cloaks, and 5,000 brazen vessels, consisted of 15,000 head of cattle of different descriptions, the value of which, at the present price of stock, would amount to about £130,000' (Lady Wilde, 'Ancient Legends of Ireland' pages 414-415)

And Lady Wilde was writing at the end of the 19th century! Cattle indeed were wealth beyond measure! A status symbol! A who-was-who in ancient Irish society!

Also from the King's Palace mound the *Eiscir Riada* is clearly visible. The

Eiscir Riada is a collection of eskers that passes through the counties of Dublin, Meath, Kildare, Westmeath, Offaly, Leitrim, Longford, Roscommon and Galway. A large remnant of the esker exists in the Teernacreeve region of Westmeath, and stretches from Kilbeggan to Tyrrellspass.

The Eiscir Riada, composed of sand, gravel and boulders, was formed back in the ice age, when the ice pushed the land up into a peak, and as the ice melted, the ridge was left that runs across the country from east to west, - Dublin to Galway. Around 10,000 years ago!

The Irish name 'Eiscir Riada' provides an indication of the significance of the eskers, 'Eiscir' meaning 'divide' and 'Riada' meaning 'road'.

Following a battle at Maynooth, in the year 123 AD, the island of Ireland was divided into two political entities along the line of the eskers – 'Leath Cuinn', - 'Conn's Half' to the north, and 'Leath Mogha' - 'Mogha's Half' to the south.

Because of its slightly higher ground, the Esker Riada provided a route through the bogs of the Irish midlands. It has, since ancient times, formed a highway joining the east and west of Ireland. Indeed, its ancient Gaelic name is 'An tSlí Mhór', meaning 'The Great Way'.

The Slighe Mhór provided a link between Clonard Abbey, Durrow Abbey and the monastic settlement of Clonmacnoise, constructed at the point where the River Shannon passes through the Esker Riada.

To this day, the Esker Riada continues to serve as a highway, the main N6 Dublin to Galway road still closely following it, and much agricultural activity still takes place along its length. The Dublin part begins at High Street, beside Wood Quay, where the Viking settlement and the original ford made of hurdles, or basketwork, that gives Dublin its name, - ' *Átha Cliath',* - and follows southwest through Kilmainham to Greenhills Road.

FAIRY TREE

As we leave the King's Palace and walk down through the gate into the main Uisneach site, we come first to the Fairy Tree.

This is the place of the Tuatha Dé Danann, already mentioned, and to recap, - A supernatural legendary race skilled in arts, sciences, healing and energetic *'magic'* who are said to be the creators of the great Irish monuments including Newgrange.

They fought and overcame the previous Irish inhabitants, the Fir Bolg at the First Battle of Moytura (Magh Tuireadh). Subsequently they then had to defeat the Fomorians at the Second Battle of Moytura to usher in a peaceful reign until the arrival of the Celtic Milesians, the sons of Miled. It is often said that the early Christian storytellers could not permit a pagan race, endowed as they were with mysterious and divine power, to be the progenitors and forefathers of Christian Ireland, so they supplanted them with the Milesians, - sons of Miled, - equally mythical, but in this case a wholly human invader.

The **Fir Bolgs!** Who were they? Lady Wilde explains:

'The earliest historic race of Ireland was a pastoral people called Firbolg, said to be of Greek or Eastern origin, probably a branch of that great Celtic race which, having passed through Europe and round its shores,

found a resting-place at last in Ireland. Of the Fomorians, Nemedians, and other minor invaders, we need not speak, as they have left nothing by which to trace their footsteps. The old annalists bring them direct from the Ark, and in a straight line from Japher. The coming of Pharaoh's daughter from Egypt with her ships may also be considered apocryphal. But the Firbolgs begin our authentic history. They had laws and social institutions, and established a monarchical government at the far-famed Hill of Tara, about which our early centres of civilization sprung.

I cannot say that the Firbolg was a cultivated man, but I think he was a shepherd and an agriculturist. I doubt if he knew anything, certainly not much, of metallurgy; but it does not follow that he was a mere savage, no more than the Maories of New Zealand were when we first came into contact with them........

The Firbolgs were a small, straight-haired, swarthy race, who have left a portion of their descendants with us to this very day. A genealogist (their own countryman resident in Galway about two hundred years ago) described them as dark-haired, talkative, guileful, strolling, unsteady, 'disturbers of every Council and Assembly', and 'promoters of discord'. (Lady Wilde, *'Ancient Legends of Ireland'* pages 416-417)

So the Firbolgs were the predecessors of the Tuatha Dé Danann.

And the **Milesians,** the sons of Miled! Where do they fit into the story? Lady Wilde again:

'It is affirmed that the Dananns ruled in Ireland for a long time, until another inroad was made into the island by the Milesians - said to be brave, chivalrous, skilled in war, good navigators, proud, boastful, and much superior in outward adornment as well as mental culture, but

probably not better armed than their opponents. They deposed the last three Danann kings and their wives, and rose to be, it is said, the dominant race - assuming the sovereignty, becoming the aristocracy and landed proprietors of the country, and giving origin to those chieftains that afterwards rose to the title of petty kings, and from whom some of the best families in the land with anything like Irish names claim descent, and particularly those with the prefix of the 'O' or the 'Mac'. When this race arrived in Ireland I cannot tell, but it was some time prior to the Christian era. It is said they came from the coast of Spain, where they had long remained after their Eastern emigration.'
(Lady Wilde, *'Ancient Legends of Ireland'* page 420)

So the Firbolgs, then the Tuatha Dé Danann, then the Milesians - in that specific order!

But back to the Tuatha Dé Danann again!

After much subsequent negotiations, the Tuatha Dé Danann were defeated at Tailtiu, and Amergin, the Milesian Bard, divided the land in two, above ground for his people and below ground for the Tuatha Dé Danann who morphed into the Shining Ones, Na Sidhe, the Faerie Folk, the people of the fairy mounds, who inhabit the Cairn monuments and sacred sites, portals to the Otherworld. Here they remained - as a powerful influence in the mythology of Ireland, living alongside mortal man and moving between the two worlds as they wished and saw fit. And here they held the wisdom of their ways of life, where male and female were equal but different, the land was respected and everyone in the tribe recognised and practised *'medicine ways of healing'*. It is generally believed that the complete pantheon of Irish Gods and Goddesses originate from them.

The hawthorn tree is very special, protecting the Daoine Maithe, the Sidhe, the fairy folk. And trees with rocks underneath them were believed to be a place of assembly where the Daoine Maithe, the good people, sat around and met at night. And this tree at Uisneach is a hawthorn.

The Tuatha Dé Danann, retreating underground, promised they would come back again to this world when the veil is thin, on the Eve of the festival of Samhain. A date which changes every year, as Samhain follows the astrological dates, not the Gregorian calendar.

Saint Patrick's Bed

Walking on down from the Fairy Tree, we pass the huge effigy of the Goddess Eriu herself, then Lough Lugh where the God Lugh met his mortal end, and behind which it is said that he was laid to rest in the early bronze age cairn behind the lake, Cairn Lugdach. Then we pass the wooden figure of Lugh himself and so on up to the summit of the mound, and here we find the monument known as St. Patrick's Bed - right at the summit.

Although yet to be excavated, it is considered to be the remains of a Neolithic passage tomb with an entrance facing west. And it actually pre-dates St. Patrick by thousands of years - 4000 years! It dates back to before the pyramids, before Stonehenge! And is testimony to those ancient, first people with their knowledge of astronomy, - how they could figure out the earth's rotation by building these sites to mark the exact rise or setting of the sun at any particular time of the year!

So, if this site predates St. Patrick by thousands of years, why is it called

St. Patrick's Bed? - Good question!

In the 5th Century it is said St. Patrick came to Uisneach, trying to establish his Church. But the O'Neill clan, - the southern O 'Neills, - objected. St. Patrick cursed the stones, and rendered them no good for heating, washing or building.

Then in the 12 Century, in 1111 it was a meeting place for an important Christian synod, when the dioceses were created that are still what we have today.

But it may be more because of its use as a mass rock during penal times that the monument was given the name St. Patrick's Bed.

However, St Patrick did have a well on the Hill named in his honour and a number of small churches were founded around Uisneach too.

Ground surveys have shown that the monument is surrounded by a circular enclosure, - 25m diameter, - which may be the oldest man-made feature on the Hill of Uisneach.

Standing on the highest point here, one can easily get a feeling of being completely encircled by the whole of Ireland, and on a clear day, 20 counties are visible. - Dublin Mountains, Wicklow Sugarloaf, Offaly, Carlow, Kilkenny, Slieve Bloom Mts, Slieve na Mban in Tipperary; over to Nenagh, the Burren, Sligo; Cavan, Loughcrew, Armagh, Tara.

CATSTONE

Moving on down the hill from St. Patrick's Bed at the summit of the mound, on the southwest side of the hill is a large, oddly-shaped limestone rock inside a circular enclosure. It is almost 6 metres tall, - 20 ft, - and thought to weigh over 30 tons. In Irish, it is called the *'Ail na Míreann '* - *'stone of the divisions',* as it is said to mark the exact centre of Ireland and the meeting point of the ancient five provinces, - Ulster, Munster, Leinster, Connaught and Meath or Midhe, the Middle province.

As you come down the hill, towards the Catstone, there is a noticeable rise in both temperature and energy! And of note also is a hawthorn tree standing on its own, over to your right, that only blooms on its west side. Why? - Another good question! But no logical explanation has been yet offered!

Tradition has it that the men stop at the top of the hill and the women proceed to the Catstone, and then they must invite the men to join them. And then, - generally speaking, - the women walk around the Catstone with the sun, three times, expressing their intentions.

The stone itself is a limestone erratic, deposited here at the end of the last Ice Age. It denote a ceremonial site of some sort, surrounded by a pond/ring-barrow about 25m in diameter, - a type of monument associated with Bronze/Iron Age burial traditions, - dating approximately 2400BC-400AD. The ring barrow, - a man-made rise made by the druids, - is over 5,000 years old.

And over to the right, is Saint Brigid's well, a pristine spot where modern-day Christianity and ancient paganism merge.

And the Goddess Eriu herself is said to rest beneath the Catstone - the nickname for the Stone of Divisions, simply because many see it resembling a cat in its outline.

The Catstone is a beautiful space, a place of the Divine Feminine. The positive energy is calming, giving, comforting, and when you come here, you need to turn off, to ground, you need to be present, to just breathe in the landscape.

The Catstone here on Uisneach is said to be the very centre point of Ireland, - the navel of Ireland, the *'Umbilicus Hibernia'* - the umbilical cord of Ireland, the resting place of Eriu, Mother Earth. James Joyce referred to it as an Umphala stone, - like Delphi in Greece, - umphala stones worldwide representing a navel, a centre point. It has also been referred to as the centre of the world, and even the centre of the Universe!

From every walk of life and from many cultures, people continue to come to the Hill of Uisneach. On World Peace and Prayer Day a few years ago, a group of Native Americans arrived to celebrate the event at Uisneach. Riding bareback on piebald horses, and in ceremonial head feathers, - it must surely have been a remarkable sight!

Health and Safety!

A clairvoyant, on a recent visit to Uisneach, has described how an ancient form of health and safety was observed at Uisneach.

St. Brigid's well is located about one and a half miles away at the foothill of Uisneach. And it was here at St. Brigid's Well, where everyone who was visiting Uisneach was stopped, and their water taken from them, for fear it was polluted. It was then thrown away, and their vessels refilled from the water at Brigid's Well. Feet and hands were also cleansed.

Then they would have come to the south facing side of the hill and would have gone to the ring fort below the Catstone, where they would have been searched and any weapons confiscated and kept until they were returning, as no weapons were allowed on the hill. Then they would have made their way up the hill to the summit, past the Catstone.

And the same process would have applied to those entering the King's Palace from the ancient road. Nobles bearing gifts for the king, or any others of importance would have had their weapons taken from them at the end of the roadway, as well as everything they were carrying and just left with the clothes they were wearing. The King's men would then walk behind them carrying their belongings, and once everything was checked, and the King approved, all would be returned. Because remember! The kingship was always bitterly fought and contested and enemies were always lurking, waiting for any chance to kill the king and seize power.

Bealtaine Fire

A special time on the Hill of Uisneach is Bealtaine, in the month of May. The lighting of the Bealtaine Fire is celebrated on the Hill of Uisneach and is one of Ireland's oldest traditions. In ancient times, a great assembly would gather on the Hill to witness the fire being lit by the High King of Ireland. The Bealtaine Fire is traditionally seen as marking the arrival of Summer in Ireland and a symbol of the re-birth and rejuvenation of the land after the long winter months, - a great assembly, a great gathering, the '*Aonach*' - the fair of fertility. The time when Mother Earth is now with child. And attended by as many as one quarter of a million people, and on one occasion by Michael D. Higgins to celebrate its importance, marking the beginning of summertime.

One of the most enduring legends of Uisneach is that it was the location for the first great fire to be lit in Ireland. To usher in the first dawn of summer in May, the Uisneach hearth burned biggest and brightest of all; visible to over a quarter of Ireland. Hearths were extinguished in every Irish home and fireplace in the country, in anticipation of a new flame from Uisneach's Bealtaine fire.

Finally, - a poem about Uisneach, summing it all up - penned by Kyrie Murray, the Bard of Tara:

'Upon the hill of Uisneach, / I sit and write this poem, / About Eriu our goddess / Who called this place her home. /

It's a hill of great power, / Imagination too, and fear, / And the good god Dagda, / Kept his solar horses here. /

It's now a place of pilgrimage, / It has the goddess's sacred bones / And the sacred ring of Stonehenge / Is said to have its stones. /

It's called the 'Hill of Balor' / And mentioned in 'Finnegan's Wake' / And Lugh the great harvest god / Was drowned here in a lake. /

They lit the Bealtaine fires here, / And had buildings thatched with reed, / And Brian Boru once came here, / To claim the sovereignty of Meath. /

Eriu's grave is now marked, / By a rock called 'The Cat Stone' / And a synod of bishops met here once, / To make this whole country their own. /

Giant hailstones fell in 538, / And warriors fled from there, / And ancient laws were passed here, / At the annual Lughnasa fair. /

It's a hill of great power, / celebration too and greed, / And was once a kingdom of its own, / The fifth province called Meath.'

The Hill of Uisneach has featured in nearly every significant Irish Event - political, cultural, or religious. The story of Uisneach is indeed the story of Ireland. From our earliest ancestors to the medieval high kings; from the saints and scholars of early Christianity to the freedom fighters and political leaders of the modern era, - All have left their mark on the Hill of Uisneach.

And so when you walk here upon this land of Uisneach, there is a feeling of coming home, of re-connecting with the important things of life. Of reconnecting with your very soul!

Chapter 6:

Mythological and sacred Tara

Who has not heard of Tara? Tara! - Synonymous with Ireland! Tara! - The spirit of Ireland! The famous Hill of Tara, in the Boyne River Valley, - the great river which is named for the Irish goddess Boann.

There is no such thing as chance or coincidence, and so the selection of this site of Tara by whatever peoples first constructed and inhabited it was a deliberate choice. From the vantage point of the Hill of Tara, one has a clear view out to the horizon in all four directions. It was from this Hill of Tara that the island of Ireland was ruled at various stages down through history. Tara is not just an ancient hill fort, associated with ancient legends and myths, ancient kings and queens, ancient gods and goddesses, but also a place of pilgrimage, ceremony and meditation, a place where people come from all over the world to connect with the sacred land, to touch and feel the living energies that run under and on the landscape here, and to renew that deep spiritual connection which we all seek with our inner world, that communion with those other invisible forces that surround and inter-penetrate our physical world.

Many who visit Tara come back time and time again, - feeling various sensations and emotions stirred up deep within, as they absorb the high-power energy, and go away feeling re-connected, anchored, relieved of worldly worries and problems, with a more expansive perspective on life and a greater awareness that there is much, much more above and beyond our very limited third dimension energy level.

In Seamus Heaney's words: *'If ever there was a place that deserved to be preserved in the name of the dead generations from pre-historic times to historic times up to completely recently - it was Tara.'*

The name Tara itself is the English version of the Old Irish **Temair,** that has as its root **Tem,** meaning *'to cut'* or *'to set apart'*. This refers to a space set apart or cut off for sacred purposes. And the Greek word **Temenos** means a sacred place defined by a ditch, boundary stones, or an enclosing wall, and the Latin word **Templum** means *'sacred precinct'* or *'Place of great prospect'*. And then there was Tea Tephi, an Egyptian Queen, who married the King of Tara. Many would say that Tara is named after her, - and that her resting place is a little mound on Tara.

Tara is commemorated in songs and poetry. Probably the best-known song is Thomas Moore's *'The Harp That Once Through Tara's Halls',* 1821:

'The harp that once, through Tara's halls, / The soul of music shed, / Now hangs as mute on Tara's walls / As if that soul were fled.— / So sleeps the pride of former days, / So glory's thrill is o'er, / And hearts, that once beat high for praise, / Now feel that pulse no more!

No more to chiefs and ladies bright / The harp of Tara swells; / The chord, alone, that breaks at night, / Its tale of ruin tells. / Thus Freedom now so seldom wakes, / The only throb she gives, / Is when some heart indignant breaks, / To shew that still she lives!'

And we find the poem *'Song of Tara'* in a tenth century manuscript:

'There is a hill on this fair land / T'was never owned and never can, /And from its prow the eye can see / The very ends of Innishfree. / Here once stood the Royal Seat / And here once trod the Fianna feet. /Silent now

but not forlorn / For this is still the Ard Riogh's home. /Cernait, Grainne, Cormac, Fionn, / T'was here they loved and lost and won. / Their secrets lie 'neath Tara's soil, / Known only to the Lia Fail.'

Tara has been at the centre of political events right down through history. It was a Celtic site, - one of the largest complexes of Celtic monuments in all of Europe. The first settlers came about 6000 years ago. They chose Tara as a very special site, because of the energy line of the earth. Tara has always been a sacred place, a Royal place, and a Celtic place.

As a sacred place in ancient Irish religion and mythology, Tara was revered as a dwelling of the gods and an entrance place to the Otherworld of eternal joy and plenty where no mortal ever grew old. In the legends of St. Patrick's mission to Ireland he is said to have come first to Tara in order to confront the ancient religion in its most powerful site.

As a a royal site in prehistory and in historic times, 142 kings are said to have reigned in the Name of Tara. It is an important archaeological site in Ireland and worldwide. Use of the site dates from prehistory to the present. Monuments range from approx. 3500 BC to 400 AD. The site was mainly used in prehistory for ritual and religious purposes and as a cemetery, but there is also evidence of settlement.

And to put Tara into historical perspective! - The Mound of the Hostages was built c 3500 BC; the Great Pyramid of Giza was completed 2600 BC; Stonehenge 2200 -1800 BC and Julius Caesar attacked Britain 55 B.C. That's how ancient Tara actually is!

And it was at Tara that the most powerful of Irish kings held their inaugural feasts and honoured the Earth Mother Goddess Maeve.

And in more recent centuries?

During the 1641 rebellion in Ulster, Tara was the location of rebel meetings. And during the 1798 Wolfe Tone and United Irishmen rebellion, 350 rebels were said to have been killed in the Battle of Tara. A stone to commemorate the men who died in 1798 was erected in 1938. The battle was lost, and the reason? - The old road to Dublin went by Tara. The British re-directed a load of whiskey along the road, which was seized by the rebels, and drunk. The result? Next day the insurgents were off their heads, ran out after the horsemen and were slaughtered.

Then in 1843, Daniel O'Connell held one of his monster meetings at Tara in his aim to pressurise the British Government to repeal the 1800 Act of Union. Tara was chosen for its status in Irish History, and according to the Nation newspaper, over one million people attended the event.

And most recently, in the late 1900s, much opposition was aroused not only in Ireland but world-wide, over the Irish Government's proposed plans to build the new M3 motorway right through Tara. Famous writers, artists, musicians and actors all got involved to prevent the road being built. In 2005, at the Summer Solstice, 21st June, thousands of ordinary people assembled at Tara.

Then In 2007, The Fianna Fail Government brought in the Monuments Act, - decreeing that if a mound stood in the way of an approved road, that mound can be knocked down. A vigil fire was lit in 2007 and kept lit day and night for several years. Protestors stood in front of machines in order to prevent the road happening. The anger was heightened not just by the fact that there was a perfectly feasible alternative route along the old disused railway line which would have by-passed Tara, but also the corruption that went on with Government members and friends buying up land in Tara, knowing there was going to be a motorway built there. But the whole event served to highlight how important Tara is to people all around the world, - with Native Americans and Aborigines joining the protest, - they too having suffered by having their lands taken from them.

And many would say that the old curse of Tara came back to bite the Fianna Fail party! The old curse declaring that if a king did anything against Tara, he would lose all his power. It could be said that Bertie Ahern and his Fianna Fail cohorts were at their most powerful at that time, but after they went into Tara, and at the next election, their power was gone, and even still today, it might appear they are clinging to Fine Gael to survive.

Nobody crosses Tara without paying for it! Or so the story goes!

So what are the myths and legends associated with Tara? And what are the lessons and teachings we need to find embedded in those metaphorical tales?

Any visit to Tara probably starts at the **Banqueting Hall** area, a long green strip just to the right over the first slope inside the main entrance gate. This was first a roadway, the ceremonial entrance to Tara, and then later became a banqueting hall. And we read in the previous chapter how important feasts and banquets were in the hospitality that was part of any king's responsibility.

The 'Book of Leinster' describes the banqueting hall at Tara as being 300 feet in measurement and that it had 150 sections, with great detail given to the portion of food that should be given to each category of guest.

And Patrick Weston Joyce 1827-1914, wrote:

'Among the higher classes great care was taken to seat family and guests at table in the order of rank; and any departure from the established usage was sure to lead to quarrels. The king was always attended at banquets by his subordinate kings, and by other lords and chiefs. Those on his immediate right and left had to sit at a respectful distance. While King Corman MacArt sat at dinner, fifty military guards remained standing near him.' (P. W. Joyce, *'The Story of Ancient Irish Civilization'* page 48)

The story goes here that when you walk up the banquet hall, up towards the Church and where the Temple once stood, you leave your negative energy behind. But actually, when you reach the end of the banquet hall, there is a major ley-line going right across and down to the left to where the statue of St. Patrick now stands. St. Patrick being placed on the energy line raised some opposition, as it was considered he was blocking the flow of energy!

If you have a metal detector, and walk up the line through the banquet hall, there is metal underneath, as shown by the needle going up in the detector, probably coming from Tara mines, but when you cross the ley line, the needle goes right down again, indicating that there is no metal at this part. So losing your negative energy means you are walking over lead and by coming to the clear ground, and the Temple, you are in a non-negative area.

The **Temple** itself would have been surrounded by a barricade, offering sanctuary and refuse. The steps into the graveyard mark the edge of the old Temple. A further ley line runs right through what would have been the centre of the Temple, and right up to the altar of the present church. When the Christians arrived, they used the pagan energy and when the priest stood at the altar and held up a gold chalice, he picked up on that energy and the result was that people could see a bright aura around him. The Christian feast days simply replaced the original pagan feast days, based around the natural yearly movements of the earth around the sun.

Mound of She Hirlings: Across from the Temple, the mound of the She Hirlings was named after the female warriors of Tara.

Mound of the Hostages: This the oldest visible ancient ritual and burial mound on the Hill, dating back to about 2,500 B.C. It is known as an old pagan clock, as the symbols, including spirals, on the engraved stone just inside the entrance, relate to the sacred Celtic festivals and are thought to have images of the sun, moon and stars. The sun shines in at Imbolc, 4th February and at Samhain on 6th November, and on these precise dates, the reflection of the sun shines on the exact center of the stone. In the 1950s the Mound of the Hostages was excavated. The yellow clay stones were taken off and replaced with top soil. Yellow clay will hold its own, and is used for building houses, but when organic top soil was put here, after a short while, it subsided and spread out causing destruction. While work was being done, the lentil was broken a new lentil put in with stone brought from Galway. These recent stones put in a few years ago are completely out of character.

The name Mound Of the Hostages comes from the custom of over-kings like those at Tara retaining important personages from subject kingdoms to ensure their submission.

In a later century, Niall Of the Nine Hostages, the legendary king of Tara retained hostages from all the provinces of Ireland and from Britain, -

one from the central kingdom of Meath and the other four provinces of Ireland plus four from Britain. Niall is the founding ancestor of the O'Neill dynasty that had 28 kings rule in the name of Tara 400 - 1022 AD.

Professor Ruairi DeValera carried out excavations here, 1955-1959. More than 200 cremated remains were found, some of which were placed under upturned earthenware urns with burial gifts. DeValera wrote: *'The mound yielded the most comprehensive series of grave goods yet available from any example in Ireland.'*

And more recent investigations by the Discovery Programme at Tara have revealed the underground presence of a huge henge circle, - resembling that of Stonehenge.

The Mound - King's Seat:

Up on top of the hill is Tara's probably most famous and best-known monument - the **Lia Fail,** - a coronation stone or **Stone of Destiny.** But this is not actually the original stone! This stone is an ancient pagan phallic symbol taken from beside the Mound of the Hostages and brought here to replace the original Lia Fail, which is said to have been brought to Scotland and is said to be now underneath the throne in England. Judith Nilan, in her book *'Legacy of Wisdom'* tells us:

'In addition to trees, stones were also considered sacred, especially stones used for royal inaugurations. These Lia Fail stones were believed to be the domain of very powerful ancient Otherworld entities. The very life force of Ireland was thought to be present in them and legend says they would cry out if the true and rightful king was being inaugurated. Their silence signaled a false ruler.' (Judith Nilan, *'A Legacy of Wisdom'*

page 100)

And Nilan quotes from Patrick Weston Joyce, '*A Social History of Ireland*', originally published in 1903:

'*Some of the inauguration stones had the impression of two feet, popularly believed to be the exact size of the feet of the first chief of the tribe who took possession of the territory. Sometimes it was a stone chair, on which the king sat during the ceremony. On the day of the inauguration the sub-chiefs of the territoiry, and all the great officers of state, with the Brehons, poets, and historians, were present, as also the bishops, abbots, and other leading ecclesiastics. Then, while he stood on the stone, an officer - whose special duty it was - handed him a straight white wand, a symbol of authority, and also an emblem of what his conduct and judicial decisions should be - straight and without stain. Having put aside his sword and other weapons, and holding the rod in his hand, he turned thrice round from left to right, and thrice from right to left to view his terrotory in every direction.*' (Judith Nilan, '*A Legacy of Wisdom*' page 100, and quoting Patrick Joyce '*A Social History of Ireland*')

Nilan continues:

'*A relationship with the life force energy of the land was far more than reverential and protective. It was not merely a respectful co-existence. It was a naturalistic collaboration. It was an alliance. And so to be in alliance with the land was to be in alliance with the essential nature of Ireland, the great Goddess Eriu, daughter of the Tuatha De and for whom Ireland is named. Over time human ability to read the landscape diminished and a knowing of the earth's mystical consciousness was all but lost. Yet although we may have lost our memory of her, she has not lost her memory of us.'* (Judith Nulan, *'A Legacy of Wisdom'* page 101)

Teach Cormac - Cormac's House: The royal personage most associated with Tara is King Cormac MacAirt whose reign is said to have lasted some 40 years, 220 AD to 260 AD, a time coinciding with the legends of the great Finn MacCool and his warrior band, known as The Fianna. And it was Cormac who was credited with composing the Brehon Laws of Ireland.

At the top of this mound is the site of what was King Cormac's house. It is in the shape of a bowl. There has been a structure detected underneath the center of Teach Cormac, but as yet no excavation has been undertaken.

A 10th century poem tells how:

'When Cormac was in Tara, a kingly equal of his was not to be found in all the world.' .... *'A golden age of plenty.'*

Ringlestown Rath in Kilmessan is the source of a lot of the energy of Tara. Two lines of energy flow straight through the center of the bowl-shaped Cormac's House. If you stand on this energy line on 21st June, with your back to Ringlestown Rath, and look straight ahead, you will see the sun rise on this energy line. - A ley line activated by the sunrise!

Rath Laoghaire: Named after King Laoghaire who was always fighting with the Leinstermen, usually trying to impose a tax on therm. As the story goes, Laoghaire was told he was going to be killed between Eirenn and Alba, so he kept off the seas between Ireland and Scotland in order to avoid his fate. But Eirenn and Alba were actually two peaks in the Wicklow Mountains, and when he was going between the two, he was struck by lightning and killed. He is buried in the middle of Rath

Laoghaire according to his wish, and wearing his armour, standing upright and facing the King of Leinster with whom he was always at war. When the King of Leinster subsequently died, he too was buried with his armour on, standing upright, and facing Rath Laoghaire. Hence the statement: *'The Irishmen never know when to give up a fight!'*

Rath of the Synods: Gets its name from three church meetings of abbots and bishops that are said to have taken place here at Tara after the supposed time of St. Patrick, the last of which was called by Adamnan in 697 AD.

In the early 20th century, a group of British Israelites arrived at Tara, in the belief that the Arc of the Covenant had been brought from Egypt and buried here. Wanting to present the Covenant as a present for the coronation of King George of England, they dug up part of the Rath, but found nothing except some Roman coins. Intervention by such as William Butler Yeats and Maud Gaunne fell on deaf ears, - the Israelites were not prepared to reason, and their disturbance of the mound is still to be seen.

In 2007 a wooden henge was found with skeletal remains of what was claimed to be a dog. But looking at it, any person can tell it was no dog! More like a Barbary ape, similar to what was also found at Emain Macha, suggesting that some form of travel and communication was ongoing across the ley-line that connects Emain Macha, Tara, Stonehenge, Spain and on into Egypt and the pyramids.

Nemneac Well: The Nemneac Well is the source of the River Nith, and the site of the first watermill in Ireland, built by King Cormac for the farmeress Mairisia who made bread for him. The mill was for grinding the corn. Mairisiu's house was also sited here, as was the house of Mata the monster, in the clump of trees over the Nemneac Well.

Calf Well: The water from here runs into the Skean River, which in turn flows into the River Boyne. And nearby is the Well of the White Cow, the water from here also flowing into the Boyne, but by a completely different route. And hence the statement '*The calf that never suckled the cow*'.

Grainne Mound: Known as the women's mound, as it holds the feminine energy. A place of magic with the powerful energy that comes from the two ley-lnes that go right through here. It is named after Grainne, a princess of Tara who fled from Tara with her beloved Diarmuid rather than marry Finn MacCool, now an aged widower and old enough to be her father. Their story, the '*Pursuit of Diarmuid and Grainne*' is probably the best-known of the myths and legends of Tara.

3 Chakra Mounds: Representing the head, the heart and the base chakras. Again, three different energies permeate this area, - all healing energies. This is a place of the feminine, and is used for ceremonies on occasions of full moon, the solstices, equinoxes and Samhain, Imbolc, Bealtaine and Lughnasa.

Moel, Bluicne and Bloc: In the Christian graveyard are the three stones known as Moel, Bluicne and Bloc. Moel has disappeared - probably now adorning someone's garden! But Bluicne and Bloc still remain, - known to be healing stones. When the sun shines on Bloc, a skull and a face are visible, with two eyes, a nose and a mouth, and as the shadows move around, different faces can be seen. The graveyard contains many old graves of both protestants and catholics.

So what are the myths and legends associated with Tara? They are certainly many and varied! And what are the lessons and teachings we can find embedded in these Tara myths?

Probably the best-known legend is the story about Grainne and Diarmuid, from the Fenian Cycle, known as the '**Pursuit of Diarmuid and Grainne**' - the same Grainne after whom the Mound of Grainne is named, and referred to above.

The story of Grainne and Diarmuid is a love story, a love triangle story, about the old widowed king looking for a young wife; Grainne the young princess of Tara betrothed to him, according to her father's wishes; and the king's loyal, trusted, handsome knight, Diarmuid. The tale incorporates the themes of unrestrained passion, wilfulness, manipulation and sorcery, pursuit of vengeance and broken trust. And the lesson? To what else can such lead, only tragedy!

As the story goes, Fionn MacCumhaill (Finn MacCool) was disconsolate over the death of his wife Maignes. Grainne was the daughter of Cormac MacAirt, High King of Ireland, and was courted by Ireland's most eligible chieftains, because of her beauty and wit. However, she also had a wilful nature. The Fianna decided that Grainne would be the most suitable and worthy wife for their great leader, and so the arrangements were made with Grainne's father, - the cattle tribute was counted, guests invited, and the great wedding feast arranged. Grainne however was distressed and repulsed at how old her prospective husband was, and at the betrothal feast, she cast her eye on Diarnuid, a young warrior, trusted and honoured by the great Fionn.

Grainne slipped a sleeping potion to the rest of the guests and demanded that Diarmuid run off with her. Out of loyalty to Fionnn, Diarmuid refused, but Grainne laid a *'geis'* or curse on him that forced him to agree to her wishes, but telling her, *'Evil bonds are these under which you lay me.'*

Traditionally, the doom of heroes came about due to their violation of a geis, either by accident, or by having multiple geasa and then being placed in a position where they have no option but to violate one geis in order to maintain another. For instance, the mighty warrior Cuchulainn had a geis to never eat dog meat, and he is also bound by a geis to eat any food offered to him by a woman. When an old woman offered him dog meat, he had no choice but to break one of them, and this led to his death. Or so the story goes!

So Diarmuid ran away with Grainne from Tara, hiding in caves, trees, wherever they could find refuge. They hid in a forest across the River Shannon, and Fionn pursued them over the water. They concealed themselves under a tree near Lawrencetown in Galway, made a bed at Lough Gur in Co. Limerick and lay hidden from their pursuers in numerous other places all across the land. They evaded Fionn several times, once with the help of Diarmuid's foster father, Aengus Og, who concealed Grainne in his cloak of invisibility while Diarmuid made an incredible leap high over the heads of the pursuing Fianna.

In time, and as the story goes, Finn appears to have called off his ruthless quest for bloody vengeance and Diarmuid and Grainne were left to live in peace. Fionn married Grainne's older sister, and Diarmuid and Grainne settled in Keshcorran, County Sligo where they had five children, living a happy life.

But the story does not end there! Far from it!

Fionn organised a boar hunt near Benbulbin in Co. Sligo, and Diarmuid joined, in spite of a prophesy that he would be killed by a boar. He was mortally wounded as he dealt the boar a mortal blow.

Fionn and his men come upon Diarmuid dying, and Grainne, in an attempt to save him, implored Fionn to show mercy and save his former friend by curing Diarmuid with a drink of water cupped by his magical hands. But Fionn refused. Even when Fionn's own men begged him to help this great warrior, Fionn still refused. Finally, after his grandson Oscar threatened to fight him, Fionn reluctantly agreed to save Diarmuid. He slowly scooped up a handful of water, inching closer to the dying Diarmuid, but the water ran from his old shaky hands and Diarmuid died there and then in front of him.

There are different accounts of what happened next to Grainne. Some tell of how Aengus Og, Diarmuid's foster father, took Diarmuid's body to Newgrange for burial. Others tell of how Grainne swore that her children would seek revenge. And yet some others tell how Grainne died of a broken heart, or even married Fionn eventually.

So what is the lesson or lessons embedded in this legend of Diarmuid and Grainne?

We are taught to harness our youthful enthusiasm as we take on life's challenges. We can always find a way forward if we are determined, no matter how great the obstacles. We do not have to surrender our sovereignty to societal norms or conventions or what is expected of us, if it does not sit right with us. We are in control of our own life!

On the other hand, we also learn that love from another person has to be earned. It cannot be gained by manipulation, cunning and force. And desire for revenge serves no good for anyone.

Another goddess associated with Tara is the goddess **Tailtiu.** Tailtiu the gentle mother, the ancient goddess of the Firbolgs, the giant race who lived in Ireland before the Tuatha Dé Danann. Some say that the name Tailtiu comes from Tea, and from Tea comes Tara. And so Tailtiu's place is Tara.

The Firbolgs and the Tuatha Dé Danann got on peacefully together at first, but then a king of the Firbolgs became jealous of the Tuatha Dé Danann and started a battle. And as the story goes, Dagda and Anu chose to give their son Lugh to Tailtiu to foster, which kept the peace between them for a while. Tailtiu breast-fed Lugh and cared for him. And Lugh in turn loved Tailtiu so much that he started great games in her honour, in a place originally called Tailtiu, but now called Teltown in County Meath, where recent findings of artefacts are testimony to these games.

Tailtiu lived at Tara, and was renowned and acknowledged as the deity who brought agriculture to the country, and the first harvest. But as the story goes, she died from her labours, so relentless was she in her cultivating and harvesting of the land.

And that is the lesson Tailtiu teaches us! We gather the fruits of our labours! Bitter or sweet, according to what we have sown. What we put in is coming back to us. We use our gifts to the fullest, and everything we experience in life is part of our learning process.

And another legend associated with Tara is the story of the '***Settling of the Manor of Tara'.***

This story portrays a time of confusion, discord and disagreement, when some of the nobles of Ireland had to call on one of their old, wise, knowledgeable lore-keepers to regain their understanding of the '*order of things*', - an important part of the Irish tradition. In the story the characters have forgotten certain fundamental principles that underpin society and ensure a harmonious relationship with other human beings and with the land. They become fearful in the face of their forgetfulness, and suddenly they find themselves in conflict with others who are greedy and concerned only for themselves. In the confusion and chaos and in an attempt to restore them all to balance and understanding, they know they must consult a holder of wisdom, known widely for his ability to see beyond the present turmoil and restore all to peace and balance and the proper '*order of things*'.

And as this story goes, it was the custom, every three years, for the nobles of Ireland to travel, laden with gifts, to the Great Hall of Tara, to sit in council, to swear loyalty to the High King, to attend a lavish banquet in his honour, and then to assist in giving a grand feast to the Irish people over several days of celebration. This Great Feast was a way to honour the bounty of the land, to renew the bond between the High King and the land, and to maintain the memory of who they were.

But this year it was different. The assembled nobles did not enter the Great Hall or the King's fortress, but instead remained outside discussing among themselves how the High King, Diarmuid, son of Cerball, had taken such a large measure of land for himself. One of the nobles spoke:

'*As we all know, High Kings are married to the land. When all is right in the land, the land, in turn, provides for the people. The well-being of the people is dependent on the well-being of the land. The well-being of the*

77

land is dependent on the proper order of things. Maintaining the proper order of things is the responsibility of us all, king, druid, and commoner alike. With that said, I can find no fault with the king. And yet I find that I have lost the knowledge of the proper order of things, within and without. I feel as if a fog has settled on my brain. Where is the common spirit to which we all order our lives?'

What disturbed them most was the fact that none of them could remember the sacred configuration of the land, - in other words, the four directions and what each of these directions stood for. So they sent a message to the King declaring their uncertainty about whether or not he had taken more than his fair share of the land, and they would not attend the feast until they could once again figure out the sacred alignment.

So far, this story may seen antiquated and outdated, and totally irrelevant for today's world. But as Frank MacEowen points out:

'However, how would you experience the story if you were to reread the previous section and each time you encountered the words the 'proper order of things', you replaced them with other words, such as democracy, civil liberties, civil rights, or human rights?

We are also living in a time - collectively - when some of the more enlightened principles of our common humanity, the basic and assumed 'proper order of things', are being ignored or forgotten. We must slow down and invoke the deep insight of mythic memory so that we can return our lives, families, communities, nations, and the global village to a state of harmony.' (Frank MacEowen, *'The Celtic Way of Seeing'* pages 26-27)

And as the story continues, Fiachra, son of the embroideress, was first sent for, on account of his wisdom, but he refused to make a judgement, declaring that there was another person more wise than he who should be consulted. And so the second person was sent for, - *'Cennfaelad, who got a wound to the head in the Battle of Moy Rath, that took the brain of forgetfullness out of his head, so he remembers everything, and can forget nothing.'* But Cennfaelad too refused to pass judgement, declaring that Fintan the Wise, a seer, a poet and a hermit, *'who has lived through many ages, and in many shapes'* was the only person who could settle the situation.

Fintan arrived and when questioned by the nobles as to whether the boundaries of Tara were too extensive, he replied:

'So many questions, and yet these things are easy to relate. For this is not the first time I have been here in an assembly at Tara, and it is not the first time I have been interviewed about the proper order of things within and without.'

Fintan then proceeded to relate the story of how a mysterious being, a spirit-man had arrived many years previously, coming from the West at sunset. Obviously a man of exceptional wisdom and knowledge, and he imparted to Fintan much of this great wisdom.

And this great wisdom was about the great Irish Spirit Wheel. Without knowledge of this great Spirit Wheel, - the sacred law, the great alignment, - there could be no proper *'order of things'*.

The spirit-man explained to Fintan how:

'Each of the directions has her knowledge and a power waiting there that can teach us, guide us, temper us, and heal us. Her knowledge of learning and vision, her stories and histories, her understanding of the

Otherworld, her counsel and beauty, dwell in the West; her knowledge of battle and warriorship, rough places, tempering and boldness, pride, hardihood, and conflict, dwells in the North; her knowledge of prosperity, of householders and householding, of hospitality, of abundance and gratitude, dwells in the East; her knowledge of music and inspiration, of poetic art and fate, of melody and advocacy, of waterfalls and life force, dwells in the South; her knowledge of sovereignty and enlightened warriorship, of dignity, primacy, and mastery, of stability and destiny, high kingship, and principality, dwells in the Center.'

And the story ends:

'When Fintan had finished retelling the ancient story, a peaceful calm settled over everyone present. The nobles looked at their High king with new eyes of understanding. They knew he was fit to be their leader. The High King looked at the nobles with new eyes of compassion. He knew that all of them, himself included, had been under the sway of a profound forgetfulness. With the account of the mysterious spirit-man, of the living wisdom of the wheel, and of the sacred knowledge of Mother Ireland in each of the directions, something long cherished and vital had been restored in all of them. They remembered who they were. Everyone looked at Fintan. In that moment they realised even more fully the true power of the celtic storyteller, one who heals the world with words.' (Frank MacEowen, *'the Celtic Way of Seeing'* page 36)

And as Judith Nilan explains about the nobles who were listening:

'They remembered who they were through hearing the story, their story, of balance and harmony. They remembered who they were through re-remembering themselves in right relationship with the Spirit Wheel, with

the land, and as a people. And their world stopped until this balance, this harmony, was restored. Nothing was more important.' (Judith Nilan, *'A Legacy of Wisdom'* page 42)

And the lessons we learn from this?

'Myths, legends, and stories told around the fire for thousands of years, stories like 'The Settling of the Manor of Tara', were one way our Irish ancestors connected and stayed connected with the Oran Mor, the divine harmony, and Spirit Wheel. Today, the ideas of myth and mythology are much maligned as fiction and fantasy. Yes, they are often fantastical but, as Joseph Campbell wrote, myth is history. To our Western mind, legends and myths hail from ancient times, but the only reason they do is so is because we have banished them there. In reality they are every bit as relevant today. And they can provide every bit as much meaning in our lives.' (Judith Nilan, *'A Legacy of Wisdom'* page 43)

From this story, we learn about the balance of the four directions, and the relevance of all of this in our own lives. The different qualities of each direction represent different qualities within ourselves, from our highest, most enlightened expressions to those lower aspects which we need to overcome and redeem.

Let me explain further:

The **East** is the place of abundance, prosperity and householding. The energies of the East teach us about spreading good and positive energy, taking care of the body, valuing and appreciating our dwelling places, our work places, and also taking care of others. The energies of the East also teach us that there is plenty for everyone, there is no need to hoard, no need to get caught up in a desire for more and more, but instead to appreciate what we have. We must truly connect with the '*spirit of prosperity*', as it relates to the living energies of the universe. We tend to concentrate on what we have not got rather than on that which we have got, - probably out of our fundamental perspective of scarcity. Our unbridled desire for consumerism, for more and more, and then some, - this is what is diverting us from honestly considering our internal state and our spiritual connection to our life force.

We need to ask ourselves, are we managing the energy allotted to us in this life-time in a positive, productive way, or are we misusing that energy in the pursuit of false prosperity, believing that abundance is found in material possessions?

The **South** is the place of music, inspiration and creativity. The energies of the South teach us about the great music of life, the music of the spheres, the great cosmic harmony, the great song at the heart of all Creation, and how we must connect with the vitality and power of the cosmos around us and within us and with the rhythm of the cycles of nature. As the song goes - '*The rhythm of life is a powerful beat / You can feel it in your fingers, you can feel it in your feet.*'

And it is in moments of silence and stillness that we can best feel the music of the great song of life. Spending time in Nature opens us up to the rhythms of life all around us. And it is these that give us inspiration, and awaken our creativity.

We need to ask ourselves, are we oblivious to the sounds of the natural world? How much do we notice of what is all around us? How much of the cacophony of musical sounds all around us do we actually hear? How well, if at all, do we connect with the flowing music of Nature and the Universe?

The **West** is the place of sacred knowledge, of the spirits, the

Otherworld, and the ancestors. The energies of the West teach us to connect with the wisdom and knowledge of the invisible worlds. Just because we cannot see something with our human vision, - that does not mean it is not there. The ship sails away beyond the horizon until we can no longer see it, - but it is still there!

And our television or radio channels! Just because we are tuned into only one of them, - that does not mean all the other channels are away somewhere else! They are all around us, - but we are just not tuned into them!

So too, this physical world in which we live, this world we know, - this is only one level of reality, one energy dimension level amongst countless others, all inter-related, inter-connected and inter-dependent, with wisdom, knowledge and inspiration being constantly drip-fed down from the vibration levels to the lowest, - and being picked up by those who are open, ready and willing to receive.

Everything we need to know is already within us, - we just need to re-remember it!

The **North** is the place of challenge, warriorship, testing, refinement, discipline, and facing the shadow. The energies of the North teach us to release our fears, address our addictions, and through all the challenges sent our way, we overcome our lower nature, and so achieve freedom and power, learning the difference between brute warriorship and sacred warriorship. And MacEowen cites the battles between the Tuatha Dé Danann and the Fomorians as the chief example from ancient times of the 'inner' teachings of the energies of the North. The Tuatha Dé Danann, sometimes called the Shining Ones, the People of Peace, as we saw earlier, are associated with harmony, peace and maintaining the proper *'order of things'*. In contrast, the Fomorians are associated with chaos, destruction, and upheaval. And we are taught through the myths and legends associated with both of these that we need the dark as well as the light in order for our soul to expand in the only way it can, - through facing challenges and experiencing, experiencing, experiencing.

The wisdom energies of the North teach us to relate to the world, not from a victim or an enslaved perspective that keeps us weak and small, but from the perspective that we can overcome any challenge we meet, thereby bringing out the hero that lies inside each one of us. Each and every conflict, each and every problem, each and every challenge is a gift, a powerful opportunity to work towards our own spiritual transformation and eventual enlightenment. - So bring it all on!

MacEowen explains:

'So many people struggle with addictions, abusing themselves with toxic food, drugs, harmful relationships, and poisoned thinking. They haven't found (or they have lost their connection to) a true vision for their life. The addictions take their toll energetically, emotionally, and often financially, thus depleting their life force and their finances; their day-to-day existence is often characterized by a lot of drama, conflict, tension and stress. Rather than feeling a sense of gratitude - a quality that envelops and radiates from one who has embodied the energies of the Center, - those who have lost their sovereignty are often deeply bitter that life has not delivered the things they deeply long for.' (Frank MacEowen, *'The Celtic Way of Seeing'* page 63)

And:

'A number of contemporary governments have become side-tracked

from their authentic sovereignty. Some neglect the poor and the elderly, while others dismiss global warming while assaulting the environment. Some political leaders slash education and social programs, while simultaneously turning a blind eye to human rights violations and the desperate need for humanitarian efforts all around the planet. Still other leaders pass bills and tax laws that benefit the richest one percent of their country..........

Elected officials using their positions to benefit themselves rather than the people; large corporations dumping toxic chemicals into rivers with no regard for wildlife or the people who may live downstream; military sonar shattering the peaceful songs and hemorrhaging the brains of whales in the sea; megastores buying products made in China, despite being conscious that such products finance the genocide of Tibetan people; consumers buying millions of tons of chocolate per year, the vast majority of which (as of 2005) is produced through child labour on the Ivory Coast: each represents a world that has lost its spiritual sovereignty.' (Frank MacEowen, *'The Celtic Way of Seeing'* pages 63-64)

And the **Center**? The Center is the place of spiritual sovereignty, that place within us where all the collective lessons of the four directions are merged and processed. Ultimately, the Center is about our life force and whether or not we are in the flow of the One Great Universal Energy. It is in the Center that we hold our sovereignty. And we will always return to Center. Like the metaphor in the poem *'A Valediction Forbidding Mourning'* by the 16th century metaphysical poet John Donne, - where he uses the image of a drafting compass as an analogy to describe his relationship with his wife. She is the fixed leg of the compass, the center, while he is the revolving leg, moving around, but always returning to Center.

The energies of the Center teach us to ask how we can transform that which prevents us from living according to the instructions of our soul. How can we ourselves be the change we wish to see in the world?

And the energy of the Center is the energy of the feminine. The heart Center! The energies of nurturing, caring, kindness, compassion and truthfulness. The energies of the Center are all about balance! Bringing balance and hence stability into our lives - both spiritual and physical!

So the significance and relevance of the Irish Spirit Wheel, - the four directions, showing the '*proper order of things*'? As Judith Nilan writes:

'We may choose to enrich our life journey through the energies of the Irish Spirit Wheel where each one of the sacred directions calls and guides us to travel deeper into ourselves, where we are asked to connect with the vitality and power of the cosmos around us and within us. The Spirit Wheel invites us to an ongoing dance within the turning days and nights of our life. When we open ourselves to this wisdom, we are opening to the original music that flows through all things, and we step through a gateway from the human world to the spirit world.

We may choose to enrich our journey through myth and music, story and song. Fundamental to the very unfolding of Irish history, they hold a heritage of longing for sacred connection. They speak to us of traversing realms of reality to encounter the mystical. Where the veils are thin and the boundaries blurred, this world and other worlds become one harmonic convergence.' (Judith Nilan, '*A Legacy of Wisdom*' page 46)

So the Irish Spirit Wheel, known to our ancient ancestors, teaches us, as Frank MacEeowen explains:

'.........the lessons of healthy power, as opposed to the kind of imbalanced power that haphazardly destroys life. It teaches us a conscious practice of maintaining the sacred harmony of life - the physical, spiritual, and psychological life of the individual as well as the health and harmony of the community and the land on which the community is dependent.' (Frank MacEowen ' *The Celtic Way of Seeing*' page 41)

And finally, to end this chapter on the mythology and the scaredness of Tara, here again is a poem by Kyrie Murray, Bard of Tara, this one titled *'Pagan Tara'*:

'Tara ia a sacred place / Where kings and druids did dwell / And I have got some stories / That to you I now do tell.

They buried three old druids alive / Moel, Bluicne and Bloc / And over their dead bodies / They placed a standing rock.

They were three different sizes / And none looked the same / And the one over each body / Now bears that druid's name.

Cethen was the king's butler / Who one day got in a fight / With a guest by the name of Cu / Who killed him dead that night.

Then Cethen's friend killed Cu / And as on the ground he did lie, / There came the first expression / To take an eye for an eye.

Dall and Dorca were blind beggars / who fought to death none day / And a Dwarf was trampled to death / When he got in the way.

Mata was a monster ' Who brave warriors killed dead / And Mairisiu was a farmeress / Who made the king his bread.

A Queen in the mound of Tea / And the She Hirlings they could fight / And the Hostage Mound is a Pagan clock / For the Spring and Autumn light.

The Mouse Brown was a savage wolf /All his victims he tore apart / Until a clever warrior / One day cut out his heart.

Rath Grainne is a healing place / For ceremonies and Shamanic sounds / And the Past Present and Future / Are marked by three Chakra Mounds.

The Neamnac Calf and Finn's Well / Are still thought sacred now / And we still drink the water / From the well of the White Cow.

The Lia Fail was once stolen / And became the Stone of Scone / And now the Queen of England / Has it underneath her throne.

A fire's lit near the Temple / At Samhain when it gets dark / Where British Israelites dug holes / There looking for the Ark.

Yes Tara is a sacred place / About which songs are sung / It's connected to Tir na Nog / Where they are forever young.

Yes Tara is still a place / Of Love and Hate and Fear / And I'll finish now by saying / That ye are all welcome here.'

Chapter 7:

Mythological and sacred Emain Macha

When you enter Emain Macha, you feel you have entered a different place! A different energy vibration level! And that's because you have!

Emain Macha or Navan Fort is without doubt, one of the most significant ancient sites in Ireland, a place where Irish mythology, archaeology and history entwine. A sacred site of prominence especially 300 BC - 300 AD, linked with Ulster kings, especially Conor McNessa and the Red Branch Knights, Cú Chulainn and of course Macha! It primarily consists of a ring-ditch enclosure, shadowed by a circular mound at its centre and the remains of a ring barrow, or burial ground, with a circle of trees around the base of the hill, - hazel, ash and oak amongst them.

As we have seen, myths, legends and fairytales all bring us messages and lessons for learning. They all have something important to say. And the myths and legends embedded in Emain Macha are all about the suppression, the degradation and the denial of the feminine. And the ground on Emain Macha carries the feminine energy. All connected to the ancient Goddess Macha!

Emain Macha! Macha, Goddess of the area! It was Macha too who gave her name to the town of Armagh, Ard Mhaca - the Primatial seat of Christianity in Ireland .

Navan Fort! Ancient seat of royal power! With activity here as late as medieval times. Fort of this ancient Queen Macha! *'Emain Macha'* meaning Macha's twins. Macha, Goddess of Fertility and War.

Macha was one of the Triple Goddesses known together as The Morrigan, the others being Morrigan and Nemain. She represented sexuality, fertility and childbirth, as well as ironically being a war goddess who could bring death and destruction as easily as the gift of life.

Emain Macha! Ancient capital of Ulster, at a time when Ireland had five provinces, - Ulster, Munster, Leinster, Connacht and Meath or Midhe, the middle province, and each with their own Ri Cuaige, king of one-fifth, - Ri Cuaige being the highest rank of kingship referred to in the ancient annals.

The Ulaid is where the Province of Ulster derived its name. The '*Ulster Cycle'* is a volume of ancient Irish mythology, told in the form of legends and heroic epics and much of it is centered around County Armagh. Many of the tales within the medieval text relate to Navan Fort and its origins.

And it is from this same '*Myths of the Ulster Cycle'* that we get the tale about Macha, the mythical Ulster Goddess. The tale relates how Macha from the Otherworld, the world of the legendary Tuatha Dé Danann, wishing to experience how to live life as a human, arrived mysteriously one day at the dwelling of a local man called Crunniuc, - a widow and a minor chieftain, - and began to care for him and his two sons. They married, and Crunniuc was proud of his wife's beauty, strength and agility. In time the disguised Goddess became pregnant and shortly before she was due to give birth, the couple were invited to a feast at the home of the King of Ulster, Conor McNessa, at the time of Samhain, which marked the end of the Celtic year and celebrated the harvest.

Macha, heavily pregnant, was not in any condition to attend, and warned her husband not to talk about her or their life together. However, after a few drinks, Crunniuc began to brag about his pregnant wife's athletic prowess. The King grew angry and ordered Macha to be brought, there and then, to race against his two fastest horses, on penalty of Crunniuc's life being forfeit if she refused.

Macha won the race, but went into labour right at the finish, giving birth to twins. In her anger and pain, she cursed the men of Ulster because those around her were refusing to help her in her awful predicament. She announced that Ulstermen would be granted great might and strength, however at the very moment they were at threat of extinction by an enemy, they would be as vulnerable and weak as a woman giving birth. The curse was to last for nine generations. No one knows what became of Macha and her twins after that, but she never went back to Crunniuc. It is generally believed she returned to the Otherworld and took her twins with her.

But there are various versions. Some say she died giving birth after the race; some say she delivered still-born twins; others tell of how she delivered a boy and a girl, while yet others tell that they were both boys. The detail is not the important thing in all of this. The main point coming from the myth about Macha is that she herself was degraded, ordered to race against the king's two best horses, while her pleas for help, compassion and respect in the pains and discomfort of giving birth were totally ignored by the males around her, including the Red Branch Knights, - all of whom treated her just as a spectacle for their sport and entertainment, jeering and mocking her swollen belly. The sacredness of giving birth and bringing new life into the world, bringing a baby's soul from the other world into this one, the most incredible act of spiritual passage that exists in our world, - was desecrated and devalued, scoffed at and mocked by those who stood around and did nothing to help or assist Macha.

Both of Macha's prophecies came true. The place became known as Emain Macha, the Twins of Macha, and all through the Ulstermen's battles with Maeve the mighty Queen of Connaught, their power deserted them and they were struck down with the pangs of labour when they needed to fight.

Emain Macha is also associated in mythology with the Knights of the Red Branch and Cú Chulainn. Cuchulain was previously known as Setanta. He was the nephew of King Conor of Ulster, son of his sister Dechtire, and it is said that his father was the sky god Lugh. The hero-to-be was brought up by King Conor himself, at Emain Macha, and while he was still a child his fame spread all over Ireland, thanks to his prowess as a boy warrior.

And as the story goes, King Conor was invited to a banquet at the house of Culain, a blacksmith. Craftmanship such as that of blacksmiths and goldsmiths were seen as great gifts, and great gifts and knowledge were all highly prized. And so it was that Culain was able to, - and did, - invite King Conor to his place for a feast. Conor accepted and asked Setanta to accompany him. Setanta was playing a game of hurling at the time and said he would follow his uncle shortly. When the guests were seated at the feast, Culain asked the King if all the expected guests had arrived and King Conor replied that they had, forgetting about Setanta. Culain unchained his huge hound to guard the house.

Unaware of the danger ahead the young boy arrived at Culain`s house. The vicious dog leapt at Setanta, who had only his hurling stick and ball with him. Undaunted by the ferocious beast the boy flung the ball down the animal's throat. The hound was forced back by the blow and Setanta was able to grab the hound by its legs and smash its head on the stone courtyard.

When Conor heard the hound howling he remembered Setanta and ran outside expecting to find him torn to pieces. He was amazed to see him unharmed, standing above the dead hound. The blacksmith, Culain was distraught on the sight of his fallen dog. Setanta, although without blame in the confrontation, promised to take the place of the dog, protecting the pass into Ulster, and became the hound of Culain – hence his name 'Cuchulain', meaning 'hound of Culain'.

And the story of Cuchulain was firmly entrenched within the ancient Brehon Laws! Laws that were based on each offending individual accepting his duty of recompense and compensation, rather than on judgement and punishment. In recompence, and what was expected of him, Cuchulain offered to take the hound's place and would forever after be known as Cú Chulainn, hound of Culann.

Queen Maeve of Connaught too is associated with Emain Macha. Maeve is probably the most written about of any of the Irish heroines. Forceful, strong, proud, she is also devious and bloodthirsty. Daughter of King Eochaid, she married Ailell, son of Ross Ruadh, King of Leinster. Their castle, or dun, was on the plain of Magh Ai in Connacht.

Maeve had property and wealth of her own, but she coveted Ailell's brown bull, and the tale of the cattle raid in 'Tain Bo Cuailnge', illustrates her forceful, capricious and clever nature. She promised her only daughter, Findabair, to each of the kings who would support her in the war, leading each to believe he had won her.

Maeve tried many times to entice the hero warrior Cuchulain from his allegiance and he battled every man she sent. Then Maeve realised that Cú Chulainn was unaffected by Macha's curse because his father was Lugh the Sun God and therefore, Cú Chulainn had divine Tuatha Dé Danann blood in his veins.

His foster brother was sent to challenge the Ulster hero by Queen Maeve and Cú Chulainn was forced to slay his own kin, seriously injuring himself. It was this moment that broke Macha's curse and the battle proper began. Maeve and her men stole a prized brown bull during the Cattle Raid of Cooley, the 'Tain Bo Cuailne' , but on the journey back to Connacht, the Donn Cuailnge, or brown bull, met Ailill's famous Finnbennach, or white bull, on a hill called Tarbga, the place of 'bull-grief'.

And as the story goes, the two great animals engaged in a brutal fight, which lasted all day and all night. In the morning, the men of Ireland saw Donn Cuailnge -, the brown bull, going towards his own land with the mangled remains of Finnbennach, -the white bull, - hanging from his horns.

For two days, the brown bull dropped the entrails of the white bull all over Ireland. Finally, he returned to Ulster and died.

Ailill and Maeve then made peace with Ulster and Cúchulainn. For seven years afterwards, nobody was killed in battle between the two sides. The men of Connacht returned to their own lands, and the men of Ulster returned to Emain Macha, full of great triumph, and hailed as heroes.

So ends the story of the Táin Bó Cúailnge.

And there is another Macha story! Macha the shapeshifter! And as this story goes, Macha was the daughter of a chieftain named Aed Ruad, and she was his only child. She was named Macha to bring her strength, after her mother, one of the 'sidhe' the 'shining ones', the Tuatha Dé Danann, had died in giving birth to her. Her father brought her up to be chieftain after him, and taught her to care for the people, animals and the land.

When her father became ill, she nursed him to the end. Just before he died, his brother came to see him, with two of the new breed of Christianity, and spent several hours in the room with his dying brother. When he came out, he presented a parchment to Macha telling her that her father was dead and had become a Christian, and that his dying wish was now for Macha and her uncle to rule together. They were married, but during the wedding feast he suddenly took ill and died. But earlier in the day, he had sent for his three sons to come back to Ulster so they could now be princes.

But the three knew that Macha had a hand in their father's death - with her knowledge of potions and poisons. So they gathered an army and marched towards Macha. As they sat around the fire, laughing, drinking, talking about all the riches and the women they would enjoy, and discussing which one of them would be chieftain, an old dirty, toothless woman appeared. The younger of the three got up to chase her away, but as she walked into the woods, she changed back into Macha, hitting him on the head with a stone, and then gagged him and tied him to a tree.

Shapeshifting again, this time into a beautiful, voluptuous young woman, she returned to the other two. Both men ran after her, hoping for a catch, but she told them only one at a time, and so she was able to hit each of them in turn on the head, and gag and tie each to the tree beside the first one.

As the night wore on, she kept watch over them, and as they slowly awakened at dawn, they realised what had happened. She gave them an option, - either they would be killed there and then or they would agree to build her the biggest rath ever seen in the country.

And so the rath was built on the mound that became known as Emain Macha, the biggest, largest rath in Ireland.

And as a further story goes, the story of the argument as to who was the champion of Ulster, - Conall, Laeghaire or Cuchulain - Maeve devised a cunning plan to save Ailell, as arbitrator, from the dangerous consequences of having to name any one of them champion. As she suggests, Ailell tells each in turn that he is the champion, and gives him a token to take back to Emain Macha to prove it, but charges each of them with secrecy.

And as the same story goes, each man returned to Conchubar's court and presented what he believed to be the one and only champion's token. Laeghaire presented a drinking cup of bronze with a silver bird at the bottom. Conall presented a drinking cup of silver, with a bird of gold at the bottom. And Cuchulain? Cuchulain presented a golden cup with a bird made of precious stones. By the time when Conchubar pronounced his judgement in favour of Cuchulain, Ailell was well out of the way!

It is said that Maeve's resting place is under a huge cairn at the summit of Knocknarra, in County Sligo, and that she is buried there standing upright in her armour.

Maeve teaches us to live our life with passion. When we awaken to our passion, whatever that passion may be, - sexual or otherwise, - we awaken to the pulsating energy and vibration of life.

Maeve was a forceful personality, and one to whom the things of this earth were very important. She had passion for life in all its aspects, and she carries forward the message that we have a right to pleasure, and to live our life to the full, not just being a bystander watching others live theirs. And when we are living life to the full, holding back on nothing, we are truly alive, - therein lies our power.

It is through the legends associated with Maeve that we see the importance and power of women in ancient society. They were equal to men in every respect and in many cases, superior. They could own property and wealth, wage war, - Maeve brought her own army with her to her marriage to Ailelll, - and be the driving force behind any adventure or enterprise.

And what lessons and teachings are embedded for us to find in the stories of Macha?

Macha teaches us about the different parts of ourselves, to find what lies within us. She is associated with the 'cave of becoming and undoing', - the first story about her running the race with the king's horses is a story of undoing, where she suffered and was abused because she asked her husband to keep her secret and he failed, and so she died. The second story, - the story about her outsmarting the three sons of her uncle who tried to steal her title and her land from her, - is a story of becoming, where she used plant medicine and shapeshifting to overcome those who plotted against her. She fought for her land and what was hers.

So we learn from Macha that we have sometimes to be fierce in protecting and defending ourselves against evil and greed. Sometimes we must do what we do not want to do, but we will find the strength. And it is fine and appropriate to express anger at times when others drive us to it. We can be both spiritual warriors and the fierce defender and protector at the same time, and when we or our loved ones are under threat, then we can retaliate or respond with anger, if necessary.

What else do we find at Emain Macha?

- A rag tree: At various spiritual points in Ireland, you will see curious trees, covered with remnants and rags of material of every colour. Usually, they are of the powerful hawthorn, ash or whitethorn, the healing trees. They look festive; however, their purpose is anything but! Dating back to ancient pagan ways, these trees are covered in rags connected to a person of ill health. They are believed to be of the Sidhe or fairy realm and must not be touched or cut down! As the rag rots on the tree, it is believed the afflicted will begin to heal. One such tree stands within Navan Fort.

- Macha Tree: The shape of a pregnant woman is clear on the trunk of a tree, - hence it has become known as the Macha tree, after Macha and her twins.

- The King's Stables: This consists of a boggy hollow, originally an artificial, flat-bottomed pool about 25 metres (82 ft) in diameter, partly surrounded by an earthen bank, about 300 metres (985 ft) north-east of Haughey's Fort. It dates to the late Bronze Age, ca.

1000 BC, contemporary with Haughey's Fort. Excavations in 1975 discovered clay moulds for bronze leaf-shaped swords, pottery, and items of worked bone and wood. Also found were 214 animal bones and a human skull. The name is probably related to a local tradition that the ancient kings of Ulster watered their horses and washed their chariots in the pool.

Not a naturally-occurring water feature such as a holy well, this artificial pool was dug out and allowed to fill with water to create a ritual site sometime in the first millennium BCE. There is no other site like it in Ireland, although there are parallels from Britain and the continent. It may have been constructed as an adjunct to ritual activities at the nearby Navan royal site (Emain Macha), a half mile to the ESE. Or perhaps it was connected to Haughey's Fort, the Bronze Age enclosure just up the hill from the pool. The King's Stables is a remnant of a "water cult" in which offerings were made to the gods by throwing objects down into the cold murky depths of the pool.

A partial excavation of the Kings' Stables in 1975 yielded more mundane discoveries. The most significant of these may have been 18 pieces of clay moulds, used for casting leaf-shaped bronze swords. Also found was the facial segment of a human head, intentionally removed from the rest of the skull.

Offerings may have been made by dropping items into the pool to deliver them into the spirit world.

Also found at the bottom of the pool were bones of cow, pig, sheep and red deer. The excavation report raised the possibility that these may have accumulated over the centuries from animals that had become trapped in the jumbled interior of the pool. The unusually high proportions of dog bones and deer antlers, however, suggested to the archaeologists something else: were the dogs deliberately thrown into the pool as a part of a ritual observance? The skull of a very large dog, about the size of a small wolf, was found nearby at Haughey's Fort, the largest dog remains ever found from any prehistoric site in Ireland or Britain.

- Haughey's Fort: This is a large hill top oval enclosure, surrounded by two concentric ditches with another ditch inside the enclosure. It is named after the farmer who owned the land on which it is situated, back in the later 19th century. A Bronze age pot has been found at Haughey's Fort.

All the great festivities throughout the year would of course have been celebrated at Emain Macha. Samhain celebrations, for example, held by King Conor at Emain Macha lasted for several days and were written into the *'Book of Leinster'* which sits in Trinity College Library in Dublin. This feast of course became Halloween! The *'Book of Leinster'* states that it was obligatory to attend the Samhain festival at the House of King Conor and *'everyone of the Ulstermen who would not come to Emain in All Hallow-eve lost his senses, and on the morrow his barrow and his grave and his tombstone were placed.'*

Rather harsh, one could say!

Chapter 8:

Mythology and sacred Loughcrew

Sacred Loughcrew is situated between Oldcastle and Kells in north County Meath, and near Lough Sheelin, Virginia and Ballyjamesduff in County Cavan. It is a complex of monuments on 32 recorded cairns, spread over 4 hills, - Patrickstown, Carnbane East, Carnbane West and Carrickbrack.

From the crest of the hill, and on a clear day, the panoramic view stretches out to at least twenty counties, - Meath, Dublin, Wicklow, Wexford, Carlow, Kildare, Laois, Offaly, Tipperary, Westmeath, Longford, Roscommon, Sligo, Leitrim. Fermanagh, Cavan, Monaghan, Armagh, Down and Louth.

The man-made structures of stone here are over 5,500 years old, with each cairn having features and alignments unique to themselves. The cairns are all known by a specific letter of the alphabet, - cairn T being the most frequently visited. In 1863, Eugene Alfred Conwell, a school inspector from Trim visited Oldcastle and picnicked with his wife on the hills and became curious about the stone structures. Subsequently a team of labourers supplied by the local Landlord, J.L Napier, excavated the main mounds. Cremated remains and artefacts found in most of the cells were all documented. Conwell discovered 32 mounds of various sizes and named them after letters of the alphabet, - 'A' being the most westerly and 'Z' the furthest east. He added a number to some of the smaller cairns such as A1, A2, A3, R1, R2, X1,X2.

However, Conwell was not an archaeologist, much of his analysis proved inaccurate, and much valuable information was lost forever. But at least awareness of the site's value was raised, and worse destruction that would have come about by people quarrying the stone was avoided.

The most noticeable feature of Loughcrew is the megalithic artwork, as much as 5,500 years old, and most famous on the backstone of Cairn T, where every spring and autumn equinox, the stone is illuminated at dawn. Concentric circles, spirals, naturalistic motifs such as flowers, leaves, the sun, moon, stars, etc. are visible everywhere.

Spirals represent the ongoing and upward movement to higher energy vibration levels, to which we are all aspiring, while circles represent the Oneness of all life, of which we are all a part, and not apart from. Circles also represent the ongoing cycles of life, with no end.

Many passage tombs are aligned towards sunrise or sunset of solstice, equinox or cross quarter days. Some are also orientated towards features in the landscape such as hills or other megaliths. For example, the passage tomb on Slieve Gullion in County Armagh is aligned towards Loughcrew.

None of this was mere chance, accident or coincidence, for there is no such thing! Lar Dooley, guardian of Loughcrew, writes in his book *'Out of the Darkness - A sacred journey into the origins of Indigenous Irish Spirituality'*:

'If you are going to build hilltop sanctuaries, then you must start with a plan, a focus, a reason and an end to all the effort. People did not simply move tons of rock and boulders from the valleys below to the hilltops above in order to allow harvesters to move unhindered over the soil

5,500 years ago. The purpose of building was complex and planned. It had intention, it had reasoning, it had design, it had architecture and it had knowledge of celestial movements. It also had some phenomenal engineering, mathematical and artistic understanding. It was not random, it was planned and executed, in a way the modern mind finds difficulty to really comprehend.' (Lar Dooley, *'Out of the Darkness'* page 33)

Loughcrew is not just a collection of megalithic tombs, but a complex series of deliberately planned, inter-connected solar calendars, solar or even lunar *'observatories',* defining the year and possibly celestial events that our ancient ancestors knew all about. - Visible proof that they were indeed very sophisticated and technologically advanced! And all with megalithic artworks! We cannot but wonder, are these mere abstract drawings, or do they have some deep symbolic meaning? Why did our ancient ancestors devote so much time and put so much effort into creating them? And when we find the answer, we have found the link, - that vital link that leads us back to the wisdom and knowledge of our ancient ancestors.

So before we consider any of the cairns themselves, we need to consider certain aspects of the life of our ancient ancestors.

In order to grow crops, for example, they required some sort of *'calendar'* or *'clock'* to let them know when the time was right for them to sow their seeds. And so they planned to erect structures in the landscape to indicate all of this. Man made passages, covered with loose stones, and contained within round circles of very large stones were created, where on specific days of the year, the light of the rising or setting sun would enter the chambers through a narrow passage at the entrance of the structure. And these passage chambered cairns are to be found all over Ireland. They are indicators of the changing seasons, the equinoxes and the solstices. The earliest solar calendar!

In the story of Eriu, - Ireland - the great **'Wheel of the Year'**, or as it was traditionally known, - the **'Wheel of the Sun'**, dictated daily life and living, before calendars or clocks. With four main approximate dates in the year, associated with the seasons, - **Samhain** (October 31st), **Imbolg** (February 1st), **Bealtaine** (May 1st) and **Lughnasa** (August 1st), - our ancient ancestors celebrated the natural movement from one season to another with a great Fire Festival and joyous festivities that went on for several days. They personified Mother Nature in all her diverse aspects.

There are also four lesser static points, associated with the movement of the sun, known as the equinoxes and solstices, - **the spring equinox** 21st March, the **summer solstice** 21st June, the **autumn equinox** 21st September and the **winter solstice** 21st December. And all of these were associated with their own particular god or goddess.

Seasons, equinoxes, solstices! All so important and relevant for our ancient ancestors! The demarcation points in the yearly calendar! The points that determined and influenced the ancient way of life so strongly! So what is the difference?

Put simply, seasons are associated with the *tilt of the earth* in relation to the sun. Equinoxes and solstices are associated with *movement of the sun*.

An **equinox** is an astronomical event that indicates the shift of seasons. The **equinoxes** occur in the milder seasons of spring and autumn, so called simply because they mark that time in the year when day and night are *at the nearest* to being equal in length, - when there is *nearly* an equal amount of daylight and darkness in all latitudes. The word *'equinox'* itself is a combination of the Latin word *'aequus'*, meaning equal, and *'nox'*, meaning night. Hence equal night. Both of the equinoxes, - the spring equinox 21st March and the autumn equinox, 21st September, - mark the first days of their respective seasons.

And what about **solstices**? The word *'solstice'* means sun standing still, and they occur during the seasons of climate extremes, - summer and winter. On 21st June the sun is at its longest point, giving us the longest day in the year, and on 21st December it is at its shortest, giving us the shortest day of the year. Again, they each mark a turning point in the natural world.

And the **seasons**? Seasons are not caused by how far the sun is from earth, but instead by the earth's slight, but constant tilt. In winter here in our Northern Hemisphere, earth is tilted away from the sun, while the Southern Hemisphere is tilted toward it. This means that the Southern Hemisphere gets longer and more direct heat and light from the sun, resulting in summer for the Southern Hemisphere and winter for the Northern Hemisphere. This also affects the length of the days, with days in summer lasting longer than days in winter.

So, while the solstices bring about a change of the length of day and night, the equinoxes do not. The winter and summer solstices bring about the shortest and longest day of the year respectively, while the equinoxes bring about an equal amount of daylight and darkness received all across the earth. And each of these natural demarcation points brings its own particular powerful cosmic energy.

Our ancient ancestors counted the days from sundown to sundown, the months by the cycles of the moon, the year by the cycle of the sun, and so living in harmony with the rhythms of Mother Earth.

And for them the year did not begin in January, as it does for us, with our modern Gregorian calendar, but at Samhain, with an interval of approximately six weeks between each of the eight festivals.

For our ancient ancestors, the next important date in the year after Samhain was the winter solstice, between Samhain and Imbolg, - 21st December in the northern hemisphere, 23rd June in the southern hemisphere. This was the date that marked the shortest day and the longest night. From here on, the days were starting to lengthen again.

Our ancient ancestors believed that on 21st December, the sun stood still for three days, and then on December 25th it began its ascent again. So the winter solstice represented for them the demise of the sun, and was a symbol of death. The word '*solstice*' (sol-stice) itself means '*sun standing still*'. On 22nd December the sun sinks to its lowest point in the sky and remains still, or at least was perceived to remain still for three days. On 25th December it begins to rise and move north again, symbolising the bringing of the longer days, warmth and spring.

And the amazing megalithic passage tombs were constructed to guide our ancient ancestors through the 4 seasons, the 2 equinoxes and the 3 solstices of the year.

As we saw in previous chapters, Tara has its '*Lia Fail*' and Uisneach has its '*Catstone*'. So too, Loughcrew has its '**Hag's Chair',** - the focal point of this large site. It is a large shaped kerbstone, measuring 10 feet in breadth and 6 feet high, carved in the shape of a throne, facing due north, near Cairn T, 20 tons in weight, with a cross chiselled on the top.

Its smooth textured surface is unique compared to other kerbstones on the site. This is the stone that Eugene Conwell, the earliest excavator of Loughcrew, named the *'Throne of Ollamh Fodhla'* the ancient lawgiver of Ireland .

Loughcrew is the modern name for *'Sliabh na Cailleach'* and is obviously associated with the crone, or old hag as the goddess associated with this area is *'an Cailleach'* or *'The Cailleach'*. Indigenous Irish spirituality was, and is all about respect for the sacred feminine and for all forms of life. Hence everything was in perfect balance and pristine health. The dominance of the masculine energy in our present world is the main reason for all the turmoil and chaos we are now facing. But for our ancient ancestors it was all so different!

Lar Dooley writes:

'In many ways, the Cailleach is very much a 'Mother Nature' figure aligned with devotion to the land, as a mother who provides sustenance and succour to all the living beings on the landscape...........To damage or destroy any life form wantonly is to err against the greater scheme of things, and is considered an action detrimental to the survival of Mother Nature, the Cailleach herself...............

The Cailleach is seen as the depiction of the sacred feminine, a life giving and protective spirit who rules the elements and the land. As such, she is undoubtedly the supreme goddess in indigenous Irish spirituality, and predates by millennia the tribal goddesses of the mythological and mythical cycle of 'invaders' who brought their own cultural attachments to their myth and fable. She rules everyone and everything, the great Protector and fertility symbol which is indigenous to our land, our spirituality, and our culture.

The Cailleach is commonly thought of as an ancestral being of great age, so the attachment of the name 'Hag' is not a pejorative one, but an ancient way of expressing wisdom and understanding in a female of great age. She is, and was, the spiritual embodiment of the Sacred Feminine in Ireland, her energy reaches far and wide around this small island home of ours. With the coming of the Anglplanter culture this changed from being an ancient wisdom keeper to the less benevolent, classical version of the old warted witch hag who flew through the night on a broomstick. Much was lost in this cultural conversion.' (Lar Dooley, *'Out of the Darkness'* page 50)

In mythology, the winter months were associated with the **Cailleach**, - the old woman, the crone, the hag, the wise old ancient one. She is depicted as a pale-faced, long-haired, stooped, wrinkled old woman, leaning on her stick.

The crone! The last of the triple goddesses with Maiden Grainne, and Mother Danu.

The crone! One of the most ancient of mythological beings!

The crone! Connected to the sovereignty of the earth, the season of winter and the Otherworld.

The crone! Intimately linked to the land and the weather specifically during the winter months from Samhain - 31st October, -   until Imbolg, - 1st February. Associated with stormy seas and violent weather, she was, for our ancient ancestors, a force to be respected. And respect her they did!

The crone! Guardian of the earth through the dark and lonely days of winter.

The crone! Whose life is often depicted as lonely and solitary, as she laments the loss of her youth and the world she once knew. And in all the chronicles, as an old crone who brings winter and cold, she wields prodigious power over life and death.

For our ancient ancestors, it was the old ones who held the stories and the wisdom of their people and carried them forward.

And as the story of Loughcrew's Hag's Chair goes, the hag was given a challenge that if she could jump from hill to hill with her apron full of stones she would be made queen of the land. So she jumped from the first hill right across to all the others, and every time she stopped she spilt a pile of stones and these created the mounds. As she jumped to the last hill, - Parrickstown, - she tripped and broke her neck.

And as another 'hag' story also goes, it was at Slieve Gullion, in South County Armagh, that the Cailleach tricked the heroic warrior, Fionn MacCumhaill into retrieving her ring from a lake, turning him into an old grey-haired man in the process.

The 'Hag's Head' is a well known vantage point at the Cliffs of Moher in County Clare, where the cliffs form an unusual rock formation that resembles a woman's head looking out to sea, - the Cailleach gazing forlornly at the rough Atlantic waves as they crash against the rocks.

And as local legend has it, an old hag or sea-witch, Mal of Malbay, fell in love with the Irish hero, Cú Chulainn and chased her would-be suitor across Ireland. Cú Chulainn escaped by hopping across sea stacks as if they were stepping stones. Mal, however, not being so nimble lost her footing and was dashed against the rocks. Or so the story goes!

For us today, the Cailleach has many lessons. She teaches us there is no need to fear growing older, as she charges forward with a formidable energy, but at the same time also loving and compassionate. The Cailleach invites us to prepare for this final phase in our earthly life, in a practical manner, ensuring we enjoy our older years in an amazing way, - feeling free to indulge ourselves in ways we would not have done in our younger years. The Cailleach is beyond trying to impress people and beyond looking for approval or recognition. The Cailleach embraces old age as the natural process of life. The Cailleach acknowledges the gifts we have received and the lessons we have learned from our life experience, growing wiser with the passing years.

The Cailleach is present for all of us, as we all share the grandmother wisdom and knowledge from our ancient ancestors. We are taught by her to respect all living things, to practise gratitude for absolutely everything and to discover how magical a place the world really is.

Maiden - Woman - Crone! The natural process of life! And for us, the term crone, the hag, should hold no negativity, as we move forward in age, enriching and nourishing others, using our voice to speak out with love, compassion and wisdom, taking action to awaken those around us, and holding the light for all as they continue on their own individual spiritual journey.

Unfortunately, the 'Cailleach' is no longer respected as our ancient ancestors respected her. She has become identified as the 'Witch' of modern times. Dooley writes:

'Life was real back then, and spirit enveloped the land. The Cailleach became a different entity. She had slowly morphed from being Mother Earth, to being the wicked witch.....

The witches burnt at the stake were wise women and healers, and very

*much synonymous with the Irish 'Bean Feasa', or woman of wisdom,
whose focus was on herbal healing and the use of sacred ceremony as
part of the healing process.......*

*The Cailleach ruled these hills, and ruled the cairns all around them. But
her image had undergone a total shift. Her spirit left many wary of
coming here, especially in the dead of night, or even waiting for the sun
to set. The culture of medieval England had come to roost. The
Cailleach, much beloved by generations of our ancestry and our spiritual
Grandmother had forever changed. Her image as the Guardian spirit
who guided our ancestors here was gone. She had become a witch to be
feared.'* (Lar Dooley, *'Out of the Darkness - A sacred journey into the
origins of Indigenous Irish Spirituality'* pages 124-125)

Cairn T dominates the crest of the hill, and is the most visited cairn in
the entire complex. It is orientated due east and aligned to the two
equinoxes, 21st March and 21st September, that time when daylight
and dark are equal. The chamber is cruciform in shape, with some of
the original corbel intact. This cairn is one of the most adorned with
megalithic art. The light of the rising equinox sun illuminates three
naturalistic carvings on the back stone, which Dooley refers to as *'The
Celestial Ceiling'*. A flower symbol is first outlined and over a period of
one hour, this rectangle of light moves slowly in a diagonal direction
across the back stone. The second carving illuminated is a simple sun
figure such as any young child might draw. The final carving caught by
the moving rays resembles the first, - a flower, but with the addition of
a carved crown or crest on it, which would seem to indicate a crowning
or honouring of the sun god. The final symbol illuminated is a wheeled
sun carved on the right hand side of the protecting sill stone of the

centre chamber. Conwell found many artefacts in Cairn T, including some charred bones and many decorated items of stone and bone.

Dooley believes that Cairn T is, in many ways, a celebration of a hugely feminine monument, - womb-like in its internal structure, - a celebration of equality, as it celebrates that time of year when daylight and darkness are equal. He maintains that deep within the chamber of Cairn T, when one sits in peace and serenity, one enters and is at peace in the womb of the Cailleach. He writes:

'The Cailleach may be depicted deep within 'Cairn T', for there is a very fresh looking and highly carved stone, beautiful in its detail. It is hidden from view, from those who do not feel the need to seek it out. Spirituality differs from religion in that it has no public persona, no need for grandiose cathedrals or golden chalices. It is about inner humility, grace and respect.' (Lar Dooley, *'Out of the Darkness'* page 77)

Cairn T may also symbolise that within us all there is a balance of both masculine and feminine energy which we must embrace in order to move forward with respect to the greater being or energy which created not only this world we live in, but the great expanse of beings which inhabit this Earth.

Cairn S is close to Cairn T. Cairn S is unlike most of the other cairns, as it has a small y-shaped chamber, and a different alignment, - towards the west, - a sunset alignment rather than a sunrise one, celebrating the ending of the day, but at the same time the brightness of the moon. This particular orientation would suggest a cross quarter day evening alignment, at Bealtaine in early May and Lughnasa in early August.

Cairn L is aligned to the sunrise on the cross quarter days of Imbolg in early February and Samhain in early November. This is an unusual alignment as the beam of sun hits a bright standing stone reflecting a soft glow of light around the chamber. As the beam moves diagonally from left to right, it reflects off another bright stone in the right hand cell which highlights some of the most spectacular art in the entire complex. A spectacular light show indeed! Dooley describes how Cairn L is highly unusual as it has two alignments within one passage chamber:

'One of these is with a phallic stone, a tall oblong shaped pillar of white sandstone; the other an offertory platter, on which gifts of the Earth would have been left to an Cailleach, or Mother Earth, as thanks for a bountiful harvest. I perceive one as masculine, and one feminine, or, like Cairn T with its focus on equinoxes, illuminating the benefits of tribal unity and the respect for the balance of the masculine and the feminine deep within each of us. We stress the spirituality here, and the ultimate goal of any indigenous vulture or spiritual union must be the respect for the masculine and feminine energies within us all.' (Lar Dooley, *'Out of the Darkness'* page 90)

As we enter Cairn L, to our left, on one of the orthostats, is a carving in the shape of a four-petalled flower with a round centre. Dooley explains:

'This symbol is instantly recognisable in other indigenous cultures; it is a fire pit, with four females gathered to consider something of importance to the sacred feminine. Underneath this symbol are thirteen arcs of concentric circles depicting (in my dreaming and understanding) thirteen generations of people on the landscape here. The symbol is significant in its presence, and again, a symbol of the feminine rising,' (Lar Dooley ' *Out of the Darkness*' page 90)

Dooley further writes about Cairn L:

'Cairn L has a magic all of its own, but it is also a hugely enigmatic and individual monument to the ancient roots of our land and our devotion to the Mother Goddess, the Cailleach.' (Lar Dooley, *'Out of the Darkness'* page 88)

Cairn U is aligned similarly to Cairn L, - an alignment with Imbolg and Samhain. Dooley writes:

'The atmosphere must have been electric, perhaps someone played a very basic drum, or maybe simple chanting took place, for this is quite a small and narrow passage; very personal and spiritually uplifting for those who wander up here in the darkness. It is an impressive sound chamber even when open to the sky, and a fantastic place to play a musical instrument or beat a basic drum.' (Lar Dooley, *'Out of the Darkness'* page 100)

So, from looking at just these 4 cairns, - Cairn T, Cairn S, Cairn L and Cairn U, - and the Hag's Chair, it is obvious that Loughcrew has a lot to do with the divine feminine energy, and how our ancient ancestors lived their lives in an understanding that the Mother Goddess was supreme over everyone and everything.

Why do people come to visit Loughcrew? For many reasons! The peace and quiet, the scenery and spectacular views, the get-away-from-it-all experience, - yes, they are certainly attractions that draw people. But more important in pulling power is the connection one feels with Ireland's ancient past, the world of our ancient ancestors. A world clearly made visible to us and evidenced through the many decorated stones and the exact solar alignments of the various cairns, - evidence indeed that our ancient ancestors were tuned into the natural cycles of the year and Mother Earth. The beautiful and intriguing artwork, and the spectacular solar light shows that occur throughout the year must surely cause us to stop and connect with our ancient ancestors and strive to understand whatever it was that they were doing with all of this.

As Lar Dooley writes:

'As we climb these hills in the morning, we are called upon to give thanks to the ancestors. Those who understand the sacred nature and the sanctity climb early, and prepare for an event which is indelibly marked on their subconscious. They sit in peace, little bands of conscious awareness, facing toward the slowly lightening sky. Waiting. Soon the light show will begin, and the purpose of all these structures will become immediately apparent. The carving of so many stones with geometric and symbolic art marks this culture as highly spiritual.' (Lar Dooley, *'Out of the Darkness'* page 31)

And therein lies the explanation! - The word *'spiritual'*, - *'spiritual culture'* and what it means.

Religion and spirituality are two very different things. Religion is man made. Spirituality is a deep connection each person must find for himself, - a deep connection with the land, with the Oneness of everything, and respect for all forms of life within that Oneness. Religion generally does not recognise the right of other forms of life, or even indigenous human forms to exist in peaceful harmony with Mother Earth. But a great awakening is taking place, as more and more people realise that religion is much more about dividing rather than unifying, - dividing us from each other, from our fundamental God essence, and from the greater universe and cosmos to which we all belong and of which we are all an integral part.

And the main lesson we take away from Loughcrew? - It must surely be that we can return to being a spiritual culture! A spiritual culture being one which recognises that everything comes from the feminine, Mother Earth, in all her diverse goddess forms, and hence we celebrate, respect and acknowledge the feminine in all her goddess forms:

'We are all borne of woman and we should try to understand that in ancient times the feminine was celebrated and women were considered sacred, and to be protected at all costs. The Neolithic female goddesses are all benevolent and caring figures; whereas the warrior-queen archetypes like Morrigan, Macha or the legendary Queen Maeve belong to a mythology which was developed thousands of years later and by a completely different culture.' (Lar Dooley, ' *Out of the Darkness*' page 48)

Dooley maintains that Loughcrew makes us understand that '*only in silence can a voice be heard, only in death can life commence; that only by awareness of the Darkness can we choose to step into the Light.*' (Lar Dooley *'Out of the Darkness'* page 106)

Chapter 9:

Mythological and sacred Newgrange

Egypt has its pyramids, England its Stonehenge. And Ireland? - Ireland has Newgrange. - That says it all in the proverbial nutshell!

Newgrange is a megalithic monument, 5,200 years old, fashioned by an ancient, but advanced agrarian society, so skilled and knowledgeable in astronomy, construction and engineering, that they could unite heaven and earth in the most spectacular fashion, - the dark interior of this palace of the gods, associated with the mythical Tuatha Dé Danann, being illuminated by the rising sun on the morning of the shortest day of the year, Winter Solstice, 21st December.

Newgrange is the expression, in visible form for all to see, of a highly technologically advanced race, - our ancient ancestors, living in the Boyne Valley and marking the ongoing and eternal cycles of the sun, moon and stars and the inter-connectedness of everything in the entire cosmos. It is obvious that these ancient ancestors possessed an innate cosmic wisdom, and that they were aware of the divine sense of the connectedness of all things in the universe, and their own place in the grand scheme of things.

And the difference in Newgrange and other sacred sites such as Loughcrew and Sliabh na Caillighe in Meath and Knocknarea in Sligo? - The Boyne sites are larger than those in Loughcrew and Sligo, and they were not built on tops of hills and mountains. The builders of Newgrange, Knowth and Dowth were therefore able to build bigger monuments simply because they did not have to haul huge amounts of stones and boulders up to such great heights as Loughcrew or Knochnarea.

And why do so many people continue to visit Newgrange? Obviously to connect or to re-connect with the deep and profound spirituality that Newgrange epitomises. More than the history books can ever do, this monument at Newgrange tells us of the life of our ancient ancestors, - how they harnessed the cosmic forces to help them determine the times and dates throughout the year that they needed to know in order to be able to carry on their farming activities.

It is the winter solstice at Newgrange that is heralded across the world as a remarkable achievement of ancient engineering and our ancient ancestors' knowledge of astronomy. With enormous stones, the builders of Newgrange cleverly created, to their exact specifications, an aperture which admitted just a very thin beam of sunlight onto the chamber floor. But it was not just the sun that was utilised, but also the moon and the stars. Simply because if it was only the sun that was utilised, then what would have happened if the time of a solstice was missed because the sky was cloudy for a week or more? It would have been back to guessing, - and there was no guessing about any of this! This was precise, deliberate mathematical design and calculation, and hence the moon and stars were also utilised. And that's what makes Newgrange so mind-boggling to us today.

As Anthony Murphy points out:

'How many people today know, for instance, that the sun rises in the northeast on the longest days of the year, and the southeast on the shortest? How many know that the moon goes through a monthly cycle, growing from a thin crescent to a half moon to a full moon and then

*waning back to a half moon and down to a slender crescent before
disappearing for a few days? How many know that the moon completes
a loop through the sky, doing what it takes the sun a year to do, in just
27 days? How many know that the twelve constellations of stars, which
we refer to as the Zodiac, form the backdrop against which the sun,
moon and planets pass as they wander through the sky?*

*The answer, of course, is 'not many'. And that is unfortunate. We have
allowed ourselves to become parted from nature and its innate rhythms.
We still perceive the cycles of nature, mainly the seasons, although it's
hard not to in Ireland because of the often inclement nature of our
weather. We do still understand that the days are long in summer and
the days are short in winter, but beyond that people today have little
grasp of the cosmic cycles. Part of the reason for this is down to our own
time-keeping devices, the wrist watches and the clocks which are an
everyday part of our general attire these days. Every mobile phone has a
clock and a calendar on it, and a great majority of people own mobile
phones. So with such powerful aids at our disposal, why would we need
to take notice of what's going on in the sky?*

*Such a flippant dismissal of the importance of the sky cycles would have
been lethal in the Neolithic.'* (Anthony Murphy, *'Newgrange -
Monument to Immortality'* page 64)

And why was it of such importance to our ancient ancestors to be aware
and cognisant of the movement of the heavenly bodies? Why did they
need to know when the days were lengthening and when they were
shortening?

Simply because knowing that the sun's course through the year was
cyclical, repetitive and hence predictable, - this was of fundamental
importance to a society based on agriculture, a society planting crops

and keeping cattle.

And it was the monument of Newgrange that told them all of this! This was their clock and calendar all in one. The eternal rhythm of the cosmic cycles and the enduring continuance of the patterns they observed in the skies above them, - this was what they relied on for their very existence. The shortening of the beam of light that they witnessed in the passage meant that the year had indeed turned again, and the sun was once more beginning to strengthen, bringing longer, brighter days.

And what about the myths and legends associated with Newgrange?

As the story goes, the owner of Newgrange, the god Aonghus, was said to have taken the form of a swan when he fell in love with the swan maiden Caer Iobharmheith. The story relates how after finding Caer at a lake in Tipperary, Aonghus was transformed into a swan and they flew together to Bru na Boinne, the Boyne Valley, where they remained. And indeed, Newgrange is an important wintering ground for the whooper swan, which comes to the Boyne Valley in large numbers from Iceland every winter.

Boann was the great river goddess, who gave her name to the River Boyne and the cosmic river of the sky, - the word Boinn is Irish for 'White Cow', and 'Bealach na Bo' is Irish for the Milky Way.

And as the story goes, as the earth began the process of moving into solid form from molten rock, liquid and gas, Boann brought waters from the great Milky Way down to earth through her breasts. The earth was hard, dry and parched, and the milk that flowed from her breasts became the River Boyne. The surrounding area of the River Boyne is called Bru na Boinne, and it is here we find the great megalithic cairns of

Newgrange, Knowth and Dowth, all built over 5,000 years ago.

Legend has it that Boann had a secret love affair with Dagda, the god of the Tuatha Dé Danann, who sent Boann's husband, - Nechtan - off on a mission conveniently leaving Boann free to join Dagda. Their love-nest was the giant womb-like cairn of Newgrange, and their clandestine meeting lasted nine months, during which time their son was conceived - Aengus Og, the Irish God of Love. The same Aengus Og of William Butler Yeats' poem *Wandering Aengus*, Yeats taking inspiration for much of his work from the myths and legends of Ireland with which he was so familiar.

The legend further has it that Boann's son Aengus grew up instantly and tricked his father into giving him the great Cairn of Newgrange for his home, - like his mother, going after what he wanted, gaining what he most longed for!

And this is the lesson Boann teaches us! To go after all that we desire in our life! We need to push beyond our comfort zone in order to grasp the opportunities we seek in life, to achieve our dreams. Boann shows us how we need to be brave in the face of stumbling blocks and barricades.

And as the story goes, Boann returned to her husband, who remained totally unaware of her adventure, as she kept her story secret. However, soon after her return, she desired to receive the wisdom of the Salmon of Knowledge, - the salmon being the symbol in ancient Ireland for wisdom, - by drinking the water from Connla's Well. Boann again defied convention by approaching the sacred water, a preserve of male privilege, and walking around the well three times in an anti-clockwise direction, which in traditional healing was to open up and release the energy. The well swelled up, and Boann was swept away down towards the sea, and drowned.

Another version of the story has Boann peering deep into the well, and the water was so fascinated by her beauty that it overflowed, and became intertwined with Boann, to form the River Boyne.

Remember! Legends, fables and myths are all about teaching us lessons!

And the story of Boann teaches us how to harness the power to bring about our own dreams. Boann did not adhere to the conventions of the time, and by stirring up the well of the Salmon of Knowledge, she released creativity and knowledge into the world. Abundant with power and energy, Boann cannot be contained. Known as the goddess of spiritual insight, fertility, poetic prose and knowledge, she has been and continues to be the inspiration for famous artists and poets.

Boann is of the earth and of water, she is the Milky Way beaming down on humanity, with her offering of abundant milk, the wisdom of the hazel nuts that fed the Salmon of Knowledge, the love of sexual pleasure and childbearing. She inspires us to remember the great Goddess culture of our ancient ancestors, and to assess and discern between what is life-giving and life-enhancing, and what is stagnating, crippling and paralysing.

And Anthony Murphy suggests that the builders of Newgrange might well have considered its chamber as a giant womb of the goddess Boinn:

'People who feel a detachment from the religion they were brought up with, or for whom there is a spiritual emptiness in the traditional church, might feel more at home with a cosmic or natural spirituality such as that found in the Neolithic. With the political, economic and religious

institutions and systems of modern Ireland in deep crisis, it is no wonder that people are turning in greater numbers to the shrines of the pre-Christian past for some sense of their personal spirituality.

For those archaeologists who still believe Newgrange functioned primarily as a tomb, the monument is a dead thing, and its people long gone. There are stones, and bones, and implements, fragments of a story from the lost yesteryear. For those who might cherish the notion that Newgrange is a womb, they perhaps come to this great shrine to be re-born in the womb of the goddess, to encounter spiritual forces which are still very much alive.' (Anthony Murphy, *'Newgrange - Monument to Immortality'* page 131-132)

And:

'If we accept that Dagda is a sun deity, and that Newgrange is the womb/uterus of Boann, the cosmic intercourse of the Winter Solstice makes great sense. Aonghas, their offspring, had taken the form of a swan for his swan maiden lover, Caer, and the great swan constellation of the sky, which is cross-shaped, was thus transferred into the cruciform-shaped Newgrange chamber.' (*'Newgrange - Monument to Immortality'* page 154)

And Murphy furthermore connects the story of Aonghus to the biblical story of Jesus:

'Aonghus was the divine child, the 'son of the virgin', the supernatural offspring of a union of sun god and moon mother, born as the result of an immaculate conception of sorts. His symbol was the cross, copied from the sky into the architecture of Newgrange, which was his abode. These are certainly characteristics that mark him out as a prehistoric forerunner to Jesus.........

Aonghus is not the only miracle child whose conception occurs magically at Newgrange. The child Setanta, who later became Cuchulainn, the warrior hero of the Tain Bo Cuailnge epic, is said to have been conceived at Bru na Boinne through a magical union.' (Anthony Murphy, 'Newgrange - Monument to Immortality' pages 176 / 181)

And here is the most important point!

'If the story of Aonghus does indeed go all the way back to the New Stone Age, which is not an implausible suggestion, given the strength of the oral tradition in Ireland, then it can be said that the fundamentals of the Jesus story - the virgin birth in the cave, the divine parentage, the connection with Christmas day and so on - were first devised at least three millennia before Christianity.' (*Anthony Murphy, 'Newgrange - Monument to Immortality*' page 183-184)

At least three millennia before Christianity! As I have explained in several of my previous books, the story of Jesus as in the gospels, the story of the virgin birth on 21st December, of the son of God who died on the cross to redeem mankind is not unique to Jesus, but is the story of many of the ancient Roman, Greek and Egyptian gods. They all share the same C.V.! Jesus was just the latest in a long series of gods, - Christianity being the most recent and the youngest of the various religions down through history.

And here we have that same story in the myths of Newgrange - at least three millennia before Christianity!

Aonghus was the prehistoric antecedent to Jesus, a prehistoric Christ of sorts, one of numerous, a messiah of ancient times. Aonghus was the archetypical son of God, who had as his symbol the great cross, and whose immense monument, Newgrange, was seen as a gateway to the next world.

And what does all this tell us? That the story of Christ as told in the four gospels and on which Christianity is so strongly founded, has existed, in various forms, since the first stories were told by human beings, by our ancient ancestors! As Murphy points out:

'The stark truth, if I am able to express it without fear of reproach, is that Christ and Aonghus are equally mythical - they are both as genuine or as imaginary as anyone wants them to be. The stories told by some of those who have died and returned to this world seem to suggest that faith is of little consequence to our ultimate fate. Colm Keane says anyone can have a near-death experience: ....'incorporating all cultures, races and creeds. Christians have them. Buddhists and Hindus have them too. Atheists also have them. Even those with no interest in religion have them as well........' (Quoting Colm Keane, *'The Distant Shore'* page 10)

'And some of those who come back from their encounter with the other side have no major desire to rush off to mass. Their experience transcends religion and belief.' (Anthony Murphy, *'Newgrange'* page 198-199)

So as people continue to find their way to Newgrange, perhaps they are looking for a way to re-connect with the cosmos, and to find that re-connection through understanding those ancient ancestors who lived in the natural rhythms and cycles of nature. Our concrete buildings, our encroachment on nature, our artificial night light obliterating the starry night skies, our modern sophisticated technology, our consumer society, our materialistic mind-set, - all of this has disconnected and dislocated us from a cosmo-centric world view, forcing us to forge our own individual destiny through war, violence, corruption and competition. We have cut ourselves off from nature and the rest of the cosmos, whereas our ancient ancestors saw themselves as an integral part of the vast complex of the universe. We have little or no understanding in this present day of the inter-connection of all forms of life and the mind-boggling structure and divine order that holds us all together as we move through space and time.

And it is this re-connection with the cosmos and our place in it that places like Newgrange help us to find again. As institutions continue to tumble down in turmoil and chaos all around us, we are desperately searching for something concrete, something stable, something meaningful, - and more and more of us are finding this in the spirituality of our ancient ancestors. That spirituality that recognised the great Earth Mother and her role in the great scheme of things. The male energy today is running rampant in our world, resulting in war, violence, hatred, greed, desecration of our Mother Earth, depletion of the eco-systems on which we depend for our very survival, wastage of money on weapons of mass destruction while so many people are starving and without the basic necessities of life, the power of the few over the many, a world enveloped in fear, and world leaders who see force and military strength as the solution to all our problems!

So no wonder that Newgrange and the other sacred sites around our country and around the world are increasing in interest and popularity! They point the way to our re-integration with all things in the cosmos, and our integral part in the overall scheme of things.

CHAPTER 10:

The Lemniscate

Everything is energy, and energy is everything, - absolutely everything. Energy permeates everywhere, with no such thing as an empty space. And the one Great Universal Energy, the One Great Universal Consciousness that encompasses all energy - this is what we call God. Everything and everyone is simply a manifestation of this God energy in some form or other. And the only difference in all of us is the rate or frequency at which our energy is vibrating.

Energy, frequency and vibration! If you understand these three words, you have cracked the code to the mystery of life! As the science genius Nikola Tesla wrote:

'All is ebb and tide, all is a wave motion.'

And Hermetic teachings explain:

'All manifestations of thought, emotion, reason, will or desire, or any mental state or condition, are accompanied by vibrations........He who understands the Principle of Vibration, has grasped the scepter of Power.'

And yes, just like absolutely everything else in the entire Cosmos, numbers too are energy! As Aristotle wrote:

'All is number.'

Each number carries its own unique vibration frequency, and the shape of the number is important in understanding its frequency level. And if you understand the significance of the number 8, you have the final key to unlocking the mysteries of the Universe!

Tesla wrote:

'If you only knew the magnificance of the 3, 6 and 9, then you would have a key to the universe.'

What did Tesla mean? - He was referring to their shape! 3 is half the number 8 in shape; 6 is the bottom half of the number 8 in shape and 9 is the top half of the number 8 in shape.

So what is it about the number 8 that makes it so important?

8 when turned on its side is the Infinity sign, the Lemniscate, - the bridge between the material and the spiritual world, the prana, the life force of the Universe, with its unending, recycling flow of energy! The birds flow in the figure 8. They flow as One. Everything is contained within the Oneness of 8 and within the One great energy flow.

All energy flows in the form of the figure 8, in the form of the Lemniscate. The figure 8 itself is actually composed of 2 concentric circles. And it is the only figure that has no outlet or opening, representing the Oneness of all things. 8 is a constant coming and going of energy, a constant state of shifting energy. Energy radiates out from, and comes to everyone in the figure 8.

And our Earth has ley lines, or energy lines running through it, just like the veins in our own body. And our ancient ancestors understood all about energy lines along the Earth. That's why they built their ceremonial sites and monuments where they did! - On those spots where the energy was of a higher vibration!

And that is why, when you walk on these sacred sites, you feel that you are in a very special place, a different energy vibration level. - Simply because you are!

And it was because of these same energy lines, - that was why, when Christianity arrived, the pagans were castigated and got rid of - and then the Christians proceeded to build their own churches on the very same sites on which pagans had previously established theirs.

There is a link between the land and us, - the emotional memories of all that has happened - trauma, war, famine, conquest, colonisation, evictions, suppression of the soul by the Church, betrayal and abuse by both Church and State - all of these emotions of pain, fear, anger and resentment are absorbed into the land, and as Shamanism teaches us, all are held in the stones, the trees, rivers, mountains and lakes - for those who are willing to listen and learn.

All energy below the surface, on the surface and above the surface flows in the figure 8. And on top of each of these sacred sites, we find the Lemniscate, - 2 concentric circles. Showing how well our ancient ancestors knew about and understood the power of the Lemniscate! And the energy created by the Lemniscate!

And we saw it for ourselves very clearly when we were on Emain Macha. We had two beautiful golden retrievers with us, both walking alongside us quietly and calmly with no leads. Then, once we got to the mound where the Lemniscate is, they both took off and began to run round in circles, in the shape of the figure 8. Obviously following the natural energy line! Then when we left the mound, they returned to us and again walked calmly alongside us.

Emain Macha, being a ritual ceremonial site, and like all pre-Christian sites, it was built on the natural energy lines, - the ley lines of the Earth and like all such sites, there is the figure 8 on the top of the mound. The figure 8-shaped enclosure on the top of the mound in Emain Macha, - 2 concentric circles - also contains within it other figures-of-8 buildings. And a team of archaeologists from Queen's University are on to this. They have discovered that underneath the surface up there, on the mound, not so obvious on the surface itself, not so obvious as on Tara for example, but up there just under the surface, there is the figure 8, the 2 concentric circles, the Lemniscate.

This cosmic symbolism, and that is what it is, - cosmic symbolism, - attached to the format and the shape of these buildings was of extreme importance, and hence the repetitive use of that motif in their art, jewellery and architecture.

How well the 'pagans' knew all of this! Simply because they lived close to Nature. Nature was everything for them, their yearly calendar was built on the natural flow of the energy and on the natural happenings and unfoldings in the world around them. They saw God in everything, and to repeat, why did they construct their sites where they did? - Because of the natural earth energy flow right here beneath their feet.

How did that all disappear? How did we lose our connection with all of this? What happened? - The coming of Christianity! - That's what happened! Christianity with its belief in a punishing, judgemental God, a male figure. Christianity that castigated and persecuted the pagans as heathens, but at the same time, and very cleverly took over their sacred ceremonial sites and made them into their own Christian Church sites because they knew those sites were built on the natural energy lines of the earth, and of course they took on their symbols and customs too!

Go into the Vatican, and what do you see all around you? The old pagan cosmic symbols!

And let us not forget - the ancient Goddess Brigid so honoured and revered by the pagans! What happened to her under the Christians? She was made into SAINT BRIGID and so established very firmly in the Christian fold.

And what about Tara? Just as we found on Eamain Macha, there is the Lemniscate, 2 concentric circles clearly visible from the air. Emain Macha lies on a ley line, - a natural earth energy line, running from Donegal down through Emain Macha, over to Stonehenge in Southern England on to Spain and then on to Egypt and the pyramids. And Tara lies on the ley line that joins the energy line running down the East coast of Ireland through from Slieve Gullion, the Gap of the North, and linking up with the same energy line that runs from Emain Macha through to Stonehenge, then on into Spain and then on to Egypt and the pyramids.

The circle is one of the most universal and ancient shapes in the universe. The year is a circle. The day is a circle. Life is a circle. Time itself has a circular nature. And this circle of time is never broken.

We communicate only partly through language, - and partly through symbols and numbers. Our world is indeed generally ruled by numbers and symbols, - so much so that it is not surprising that knowledge of the subtle power of symbols and numbers was seriously guarded in the past, to be used by the ruling classes and passed on as secret knowledge. But in these days of the Great Apocalypse, everything that was hidden is indeed being revealed!

All energies are transferred through the flow of Lemniscate energy -

through all the various dimensions. The concentration of Lemniscate energies correlates or manifests into energy ley lines which are picked up by humans, animals and all living creatures. This is because all living things have a spirit and each spirit has a concentration of energy known as chakras. It is when humans, for example, align their chakra Lemniscate energy with the energy of the ley lines, then maximum energy vibration occurs and that is when people feel the energy of the ley lines.

The Lemniscate is all around us! We are in it!

It is a symbol and a number!!! The figure 8. Cosmic symbolism - that is what it is! And cosmic symbolism is simply the mechanism of how energy flows through the Universe. It is the Kundalini energy rising through the chakras! As in the Caduceus / Ouroboros. The serpent, when forming a ring with its own tail in its mouth, and actually eating it, is a clear and widespread symbol of the 'ALL-IN-ALL-, the totality of existence, infinity and the cyclical nature of the cosmos. And it moves in the figure 8, - the Lemniscate.

Pre-Christian Ireland was the land of the Druids. The Druidic priests were high initiates, and they were symbolised by the serpent, sometimes called Hydra. Their knowledge was deep, profound and mystic, attached to the mysteries of the earth and nature. They were part of the earliest Ancient Mystery Schools, which later appeared as the Egyptian and Brahmin Mystery Schools, whose symbol also was the serpent. In Gaelic art, the serpent or dragon was a recurring theme. The Tara brooch is decorated with a pin in the shape of a tiny serpent.

And then came Christianity! Christianity into Ireland, the land of the Druids, the High Priests of the pre-Christian world. Saint Patrick represents Christianity of course, and the serpents represent the Druids. The Druids were castigated as pagans by Christianity, their ceremonial sacred sites, built on the ley-lines, the natural energy lines of the earth, taken over and used as sites for the new Christian churches. Saint Patrick banishing the snakes is symbolic of the triumph of Christianity over paganism.

And just as Christianity took over the Druid sites, they also took over their deities, as we have just seen with Brigid, - a highly venerated goddess of pre-Christian Ireland, associated with fertility, healing, poetry and smithcraft. When Christianity arrived, they retained the personage but changed the name to Saint Brigid, bringing her into the Christian fold. Saint Brigid's feast day is still celebrated on 1st February, originally a Druid festival called 'IMBOLG' and marking the beginning of spring and new life.

The Lemniscate is a symbol of the eternal, - it looks like a horizontal 8, an 8 placed on its side. It consists of closed loops symbolising the absolute and the eternal, with neither a beginning nor an end, - hence it being known as the INFINITY SIGN. The symbol contains within itself eternal motion, and so represents continual development and the equilibrium of all dualities.

What did those ancient ancestors know and understand , - and that has been kept secret and from us for so long?

And what about Uisneach? Yes, again, just like Emain Macha and Tara, we find the two concentric circles, - as I explained previously in Chapter 5, - the Lemniscate on top of the mound, the smaller circle where the king and his immediate family stayed and the larger circle, where the extended family would have stayed, together with the bards, poets and musicians - all there for the great festival.

The natural flow of the One Great Energy! Our ancient ancestors knew the importance and significance of circles, and 2 concentric circles form the Lemniscate. They knew how to utilise, how to manipulate, how to harness that energy. We see it on Eoghan Macha. We see it on Tara. And we see it at Uisneach! It's in all the early pre-Christian settlements throughout our country!

The Lemniscate is the movement of the double helix molecule. It is the movement of life itself. It's in our DNA! The universal cosmic shape, the pattern, in the double helix molecule!

It's in the designs of nature! IT IS THE MOVEMENT OF ALL LIFE! The honeycomb, the flowers, shells, nuts, minerals, gems, everywhere! And we too are all in it!

And we saw that movement in the Dance of the Lemniscate in our recent celebration at Tara on the feast of Mary Magdalene on 22nd July, as the dancers twirled, spiralled, circled and danced around the fire in the Infinity Sign. And the energy that in itself created!

Tesla taught about free energy. - Free energy! It's all around us! Our ancient ancestors knew how to harness, how to utilise it, how to manipulate it! For their own use and benefit! For their power!

And look at what is happening today! Energy costs have risen beyond the beyond! And those companies supplying energy are making untold fortunes! Charging extortionate prices for what we should be getting for free! What should be free for everyone! As Tesla discovered! And tried to teach the world! But his notes and designs disappeared mysteriously at his death!

Free energy! But we are not allowed to know about free energy! And why not? Simply because too many people are making too much money out of us paying for what is freely available in the air around us, flowing under our feet!

And to feel the energy generated by the figure 8, all you have to do is stand opposite someone, your right hand holding their left hand, and your left hand holding their right hand. Stand for a moment or two to feel the energy flowing between you. Now cross your hands over to form the figure 8, still holding on. Notice the great shift in energy? That's the power of the Lemniscate! And how well our ancient ancestors understood this!

LET ERIU REMEMBER

CONCLUSION

So, what conclusions can we come to about mythology, about its importance in our lives, - if indeed any at all, - and the myths and legends associated with our sacred sites?

'Mythology is not a lie, mythology is poetry, it is metaphorical. It has been well said that mythology is the penultimate truth - penultimate because the ultimate cannot be put into words.' (Joseph Campbell, '*The Power of Myth*' page 206)

All these sacred sites around our country are connected, - each marking a particular time when people would gather to celebrate some aspect of Nature or some natural happening in the world around them. And so we have, for example, Newgrange marking the mid-winter solstice, and Loughcrew marking the spring solstice. Sites like these need to be protected and guarded, for they tell our story, - our very history!

Once you enter any of these sacred places, you know you are in a different world, - on a different energy frequency vibration level! A different time zone! You sense yourself stepping back in time, - back to the time of our ancient ancestors! A time when nature and the natural cycle of the seasons determined and dictated daily life. A time when the pure God essence was acknowledged in every living thing. A time when the spirits of all living things in the earth and on the earth all around us in nature, - and that governed the cycle of the year, - were honoured and revered.

Different indigenous peoples from all over the world have come here to our sacred sites down through the ages, and still they come. Why? Because they have always been aware and recognised that we here in Ireland have shared their deep belief in nature and the spirit of every living thing. They had their own gods of nature, they worked with the earth, understanding the very nature of their surroundings, they respected the earth and the cycle of the changing seasons, personifying their spirits of nature as gods. Their mythology and ancient ways are so similar to our own here in Ireland, - so there just has to be that connection stemming from ancient times! We were all connected, in ancient times, in our adherence to the natural cycle of all life and our belief in the spirits of nature. Lady Wilde wrote:

'The ancient legends of all nations of the world, on which from age to age the generations of man have been nurtured, bear so striking a resemblance to each other that we are led to believe there was once a period when the whole human family was of one creed and one language. But with increasing numbers came the necessity of dispersion; and that ceaseless migration was commenced of the tribes of the earth from the Eastern cradle of their race which has now continued for thousands of years with undiminished activity.' (Lady Wilde, *'Ancient Legends of Ireland'*, page 15.)

And we saw how all of this ancient spirituality was lost with the coming of Christianity! Tom Cowan offers another reason for this decay:

'Living in a cynical age we have come to mistrust the spoken and written word through advertising hype, failed political promises, and the calculated, manipulative use of language in the media, not the least of which is heard in popular song lyrics. In more innocent times truth was divine. 'A man is as good as his word' was an aphorism that was taken seriously. The need to 'save face' before one's family, village, or tribal

associates was paramount to a meaningful life. Loss of face implied loss of faith, and someone who violated his or her word could never be trusted again.' (Tom Cowan, *'Fire in the Head'* page 73)

And Lady Wilde offers another possible explanation:

'It is strange that, considering the amount of annals and legends transmitted to us, we have so little knowledge of Druidism or Paganism in ancient Ireland. However, it may be accounted for in this wise: That those who took down the legends from the mouths of the bards and annalists, or those who subsequently transcribed them, were Christian missionaries whose object was to obliterate every vestige of the ancient forms of faith.' (Lady Wilde, *'Ancient Legends of Ireland'* page 418)

And Frank MacEowen:

'Though no one knows for sure why we 'forget' sacred knowledge of the past or how we lose our connection to a spiritual way of seeing and living, it is clear that we have done just that. Perhaps knowledge and wisdom slip away because we take for granted those things in which we are or were deeply steeped; as Irish poet John O'Donohue suggests, we can become so familiar with something we gradually forget it. Songs, stories, lore, customs, and sacred orientations - all these can fade from memory, and when they do we must recollect them to reestablish the proper order of things.' (Frank MacEowen, *'The Celtic Way of Seeing'* page 19)

But despite the decline over centuries, there are in our present world today, more and more people awakening to an awareness of the distinct loss of the ancient values, beliefs and traditions that previously gave earlier generations a sense of belonging and a knowing about who and what they were. Our connection to the natural world, our relationship with Mother Earth, Mother Nature, which gave our ancient ancestors stability and a sense of security, - all that has disappeared down through the ages with the encroachment of the cement and mortar of urban development, the growth of industrial nations, the development of machinery on the land - farmers do not actually touch Mother Earth any more! All of this separation from Mother Earth and the natural cycles of Nature has led to a sense of disengagement, a disharmony, an estrangement, but now a desire to rekindle what our ancient ancestors had, and to restore our identity with our land. Because it is in our land that we find our identity.

And so when you walk upon these sacred sites, there is a feeling of coming home, of re-connecting with the important things of life. Of reconnecting with your very soul!

And it is through mythology and the mythological tales of our ancient ancestors that we make this vital connection.

'The dictionary definition of a myth would be stories about gods. So then you have to ask the next question: What is a god? A god is a personification of a motivating power or a value system that functions in human life and in the universe - the powers of your own body and of nature. The myths are metaphorical of spiritual potentiality in the human being, and the same powers that animate our life animate the life of the world. But also there are myths and gods that have to do with specific societies or the patron deities of the society. In other words, there are two totally different orders of mythology. There is the mythology that relates you to your nature and to the natural world, of which you're a part. And there is the mythology that is strictly sociological, linking you to a particular society. You are not simply a natural man, you are a member of a particular group.' (Joseph

Campbell, '*The Power of Myth*' page 28)

'*...civilizations are grounded on myth.*' (Joseph Campbell, '*The Power of Myth*' page 72)

'*People say that what we're all seeking is a meaning for life. I don't think that's what we're really seeking. I think that what we're seeking is an experience of being alive, so that our life experience on the purely physical plane will have resonances within our own innermost being and reality, so that we actually feel the rapture of being alive. That's what it's all finally about, and that's what these clues help us to find within ourselves.*' (Joseph Campbell, '*The Power of Myth*' page 4)

It is in our myths and legends associated with our sacred sites that we find the clues to piece together the parts of our lives that we have lost. In each of the myths, we are that personage, we experience what they are experiencing, we learn the lessons they learn, - all in pursuit of soul expansion. Myths of our ancient ancestors and the lessons and teachings embedded within them afford us all a golden opportunity to learn, to advance spiritually, to grow.

In each if the gods and goddesses we see aspects of ourselves, - hidden depths to our very being. The passion, power and fire of Maeve; the wisdom of the Cailleach; the embracing of new things into our lives of Brigid; the innocence and vitality of Boann; the nurturing and caring, but also the over-giving of Tailtiu; the fighting spirit of Macha; the desire for revenge of Lugh; the wiles and wilfulness of Grainne, but also the determination to follow the heart and not be dictated to by societal norms or conventions; the loyalty of Diarmuid; the bravery of Cuchulainn; - these gods and goddesses are all within each and every one of us, and we must all face them on our soul journey.

And this is why our sacred sites must be protected! They carry the lessons forward for us through the myths and legends. These are the places where we can actually find who we really are! These are our real history! These are our real spiritual teachers! These are our real spiritual guides!

And even though we may forget the teachings each mythological tale carries, we still remember the story, - until in the constant re-telling of the story, someone picks up the lesson again and carries it forward once more.

BIBLIOGRAPHY

Aldhouse-Green, Miranda - 'The Celtic Myths - A Guide To The Ancient Gods and Legends'

Caldecott, Moyra - 'Women in Celtic Myth'

Campbell, Joseph - - 'The Power of Myth: With Bill Moyers'

Clunie, Grace and Maginess, Tess - 'The Celtic Spirit and Literature'

Cowan, Tom - 'Fire in the Head - Shamanism and the Celtic Spirit'

Cruden, Loren, - 'Walking the Maze: The Enduring Presence of the Celtic Spirit'

Dooley, Lar - 'Out of the Darkness'

Fitzpatrick, Kate - 'Macha's Twins'

Joyce, Patrick Weston - 'The Story of Ancient Civilization'

MacEowen, Frank - 'The Celtic Way of Seeing'

MacGarraidhe Murt - 'Strangers at Home'

McEowen, Frank - 'The Mist-Filled Path: Celtic Wisdom for Exiles, Wanderers and Seekers'

Murphy, Amantha with O'Connnell, Orla - 'The Way of the Seabhean - An Irish Shamanic Path'

Murphy, Anthony - 'Newgrange: Monument to Immortality'

Newell, J. Philip - 'Listening for the Heartbeat of God'

Nilan, Judith - 'A Legacy of Wisdom - The Genius, Power, and Possibility Of Ireland's Indigenous Spiritual Heritage'

Nilan, Judith - 'A Call To Crone - Weaving Wisdom With Threads of Irish Heritage'

Ward, Dr Karen and Sexton, Bernie - 'Goddesses of Ireland - Ancient Wisdom for Modern Women'

Whelan, Dolores - 'Ever Ancient Ever New: Celtic Spirituality in the 21st Century'

Wilde, Lady Jane Francesca Agnes - 'Ancient Legends of Ireland'

Other Books by Eileen McCourt

Eileen has written 41 other books, including her first audio-book. All are available on Amazon. For more information, visit her author page:

www.eileenmccourt.co.uk

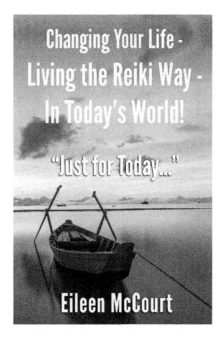

DEAR GOD...
WHERE ARE YOU?

A BEWILDERED SOUL
TALKS TO GOD

EILEEN MCCOURT

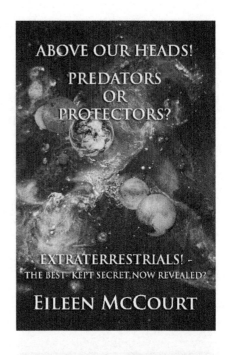

ABOVE OUR HEADS!

PREDATORS
OR
PROTECTORS?

EXTRATERRESTRIALS! -
THE BEST- KEPT SECRET, NOW REVEALED?

EILEEN MCCOURT

FINDING SENSE IN
THE NON-SENSE

Seeing The Greater Picture

Eileen McCourt

THE SINGING SOUL -
THE RISE OF THE DIVINE FEMININE:
THE POWER AND RELEVANCE OF MARY
MAGDALENE IN TODAY'S WORLD'

EILEEN MCCOURT

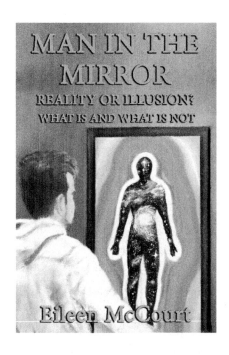

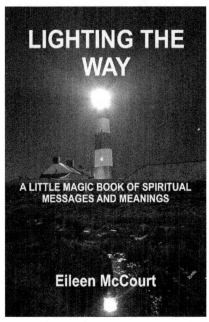

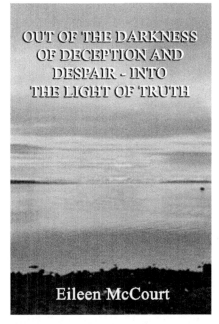

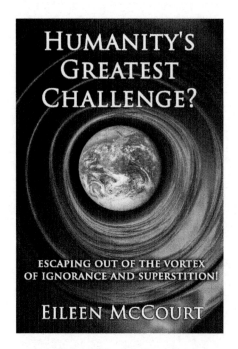

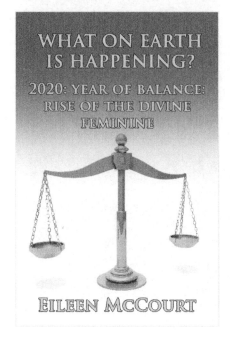

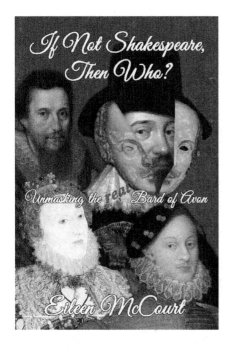

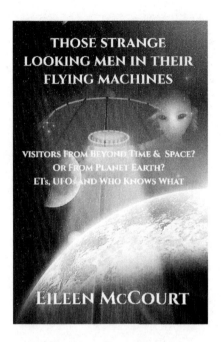

Audiobook

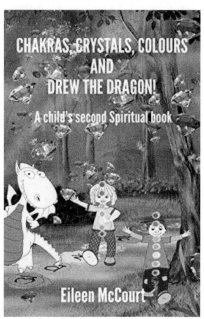

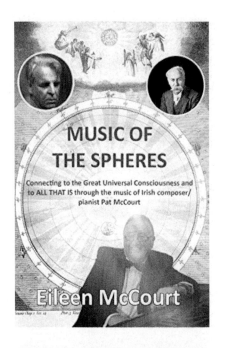

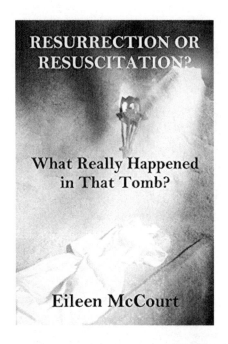

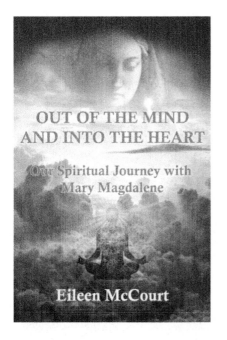

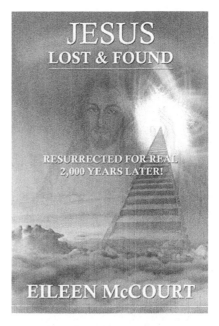

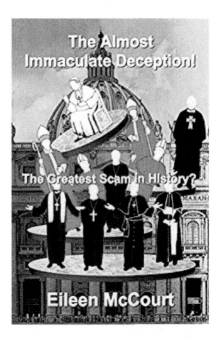

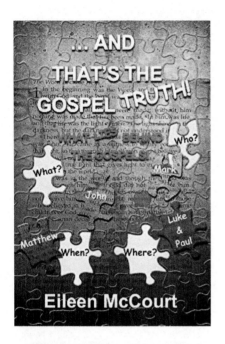

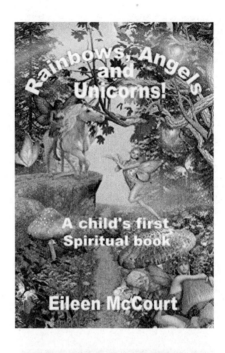

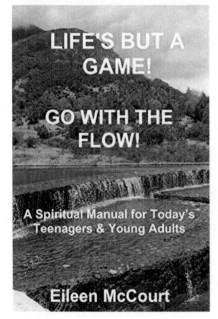

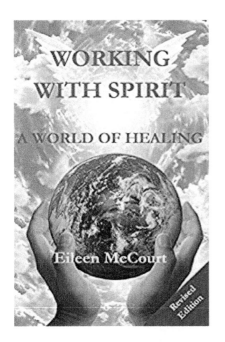

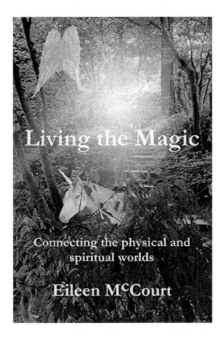

Printed in Great Britain
by Amazon

14119395R00102